SANDY L. PALM

I LIFT UP MY SOUL

Published by Dust Jacket Press
I Lift Up My Soul / Sandy L. Palm

ISBN: 978-1-953285-95-9

Dust Jacket Press
P.O. Box 721243
Oklahoma City, OK 73172

Permission to quote from the following copyrighted version of the Bible is acknowledged with appreciation: The New King James Version® (NKJV). Copyright © 1982 by Thomas Nelson. Used by permission. All rights reserved.

Cover & interior design: D.E. West—www.zaqdesigns.com & Dust Jacket Creative Services

Printed in the United States of America

DEDICATION

This story is dedicated to my faithful and kind husband and friend, Steve, and to my children and grandchildren. My prayer is that each one of you will find God's purpose in your life and have a joy-filled journey.

I also dedicate it to Beverly and Wally Walrath, who were the first people to tell us about Jesus.

Wally and Beverly Walrath

CONTENTS

Foreword vii

Introduction ix

1. California Girl 1

2. Over the Cliff 9

3. Glory Hill and Salvation 15

4. Surrender 21

5. Growing Up in Jesus 31

6. Off to Bible School 39

7. Monmouth, Illinois 49

Photo Gallery 61

8. The Second Time in Santa Cruz 67

9. Phoenix and Pomona 75

10. District Ministry and Chevette Stories 87

11. Michigan 99

12. Another Round in Santa Cruz 107

13. Arizona or Bust 117

14. Bragging on God 123

15. Making Sense of it All 127

About the Author 133

FOREWORD

The Perils of Pauline was a popular melodrama a century ago. The lead character was a young woman with an independent nature and a desire for adventure. From actual cliffhanging episodes to runaway trains to life-threatening sawmills, no day was boring or uneventful for Pauline.

Sandy Palm's account of her formative years and her family's early years bring the same sense of derring-do to mind. Tales of her overloaded vehicles and under-resourced adventures would make great sequels to the above-mentioned melodrama. Sandy would say, though, that the stories from her life were not perilous happenstances but rather testimonies to the prevenient and present grace of God at work in her life, whether she was looking God's way or not.

If you didn't know that history/English major and college educator Dr. Sandra Palm is the author of this book, you would think the escapades relayed here are someone else's story. However, over the years that she and I have worked together, bit by bit Sandy has trusted me with glimpses into her past. And I am grateful for that level of our friendship. So, reader, you need to know that this volume of adventures told by the author is a step of trust for her with you too. She'll be glad for you to take into account all the variables that came to bear on the incidents described herein. My take is that you will know you've gained a friend by the time you've finished reading this account of her life.

So hold on to your hat as you step into the pages of the author's adventures. It's an amazing journey and worth every minute. Grace and peace to you.

—*Alan D. Lyke, D. Min.*
Provost, Nazarene Bible College
Colorado Springs, Colorado

INTRODUCTION

Standing next to my colleagues at the inauguration of our new Nazarene Bible College president, I stood and sang the traditional opening hymn. Men and women dressed in full academic regalia, various-colored robes, and renaissance hats filled the platform. Black is the default color, but red, blue, purple, and green hoods gave the ceremony a regal, otherworldly look. Presidents and professors from five other denominational colleges and universities stood next to our faculty members. General superintendents, district superintendents, and pastors from the denomination in the congregation were there to give support and encouragement. The congregation filled with well-wishers faced the wall of dignity and pomp displayed on the platform.

Most in the crowd did not know me. During the time before I was a Christian, the word *dignity* would not have been used to describe anything about me. I didn't recognize my former self sometimes. Yes, I had received my doctorate in education at Northern Arizona University and was hired to be the director of general education at my college and serve as a full professor. A humbling joy in my heart and a flash of unworthiness were mixed with a profound sense of privilege to be included in this crowd of academics.

This crowd couldn't imagine the story of an eighteen-year-old girl hitchhiking up the coast of Oregon at night. Rock festivals with Hell's Angels keeping the peace and thousands of young and old hippies smoking dope and dropping LSD together are now just photographs in a history book or documentary. A congregation singing Christian songs in a small church in Portland will never know about the young girl standing outside the church brokenhearted and not brave enough to enter.

The younger me is a stranger from another life, a now-nonexistent person. Memories are sometimes unreliable, but some are burned into my heart. The happy childhood, the loss of innocence, and God's great love are unforgettable. God's footprints through my life, His protection, and His miracles of grace are foundations of my faith. His continued faithfulness weaves through the early pain of poor choices.

The romp through my first experiences with Christianity and the complete lack of dignity makes me laugh today. We held street meetings in downtown Santa Cruz, California. Beating a drum Salvation Army style, singing hymns accompanied by an accordion, and passing out gospel tracts were a test of obedience. "Beans and rice and Jesus Christ" was our slogan as we fed the hungry.

How does a girl raised in an average American home where there was love and laughter, the high school "popular girl" cheerleader and homecoming princess turn into the lost hippie girl wandering the cities of the coastal United States? Thousands of parents with children who grew up in the 1960s in the United States asked this question. Perhaps the same question can be asked today. Why do our children, even those raised in church, rebel and run to embrace evil?

In the retelling of my story there could be answers. I hope this story will honor God and show a reckless abandon to do the will of God. One thing for sure is that this story is quite different from the inauguration ceremony described above. Perhaps today we are a little too dignified, a little too careful not to seem too boisterous about our salvation. To those who choose to read about my journey, and to God, I lift up my soul.

1

CALIFORNIA GIRL

The term *California girl* brings up images of a blond, tanned surfer girl or a painted and well-primped Valley girl. I am neither. I'm just a girl who grew up in California and happened to be born in the middle of the change in American society from the traditional "Mom and apple pie" to the complex and often radical times of the 1960s.

The label *baby boomer* came later. It just gave a name to the children born after World War II when the GIs who managed to live through the war returned to rebuild their lives. Thanks to the GI Bill, they had a chance to own a home and go to college. In my early years both of my parents worked. We went to church on special occasions, owned a tract home, and spent every weekend possible doing some kind of outdoor activity. Our neighbors looked just like my family. There was a mom, a dad, and two or three kids. It was a time where neighbors knew each other, rode bicycles together, played family softball games, and went to the same schools. I didn't hear the term *working class* until I went to college. I knew we weren't rich, but I never felt poor.

My mother came from a large family. She dropped out of high school to go to work to make extra money to help her family. She was five feet tall, competitive, and a bundle of energy. The oldest girl in the family with two older brothers, she never backed down from a fight, and her stubborn ways helped her through the hard places that came in life. Always a romantic, when a good-looking, charismatic sailor boy met her at a dance and introduced her as "the girl he was going to marry," she was a goner. Only nineteen years old, he neglected to tell her that he had already been married once and had a baby with another woman. Being the good Catholic girl she was, she had no idea how it could be possible. At first after they were married, they were so in love that they mailed love letters to each other even though they lived at the same address. It lasted about two years before he was ready to move on to the next adventure. He left a devastated young wife and a two-year-old behind: me.

Memories before I turned four were hazy events featuring one-time events of getting a spanking for running in the street or standing in my crib trying to escape. When I was four, my mother and I married Frank—at least that's what I told everyone. He was a friend of my Uncle Tom and had known my mother since she was about fourteen. Back from the Korean Conflict, he realized the little sister had grown up and now had a vivacious brown-eyed daughter who wrapped him around her little finger. He was hopelessly in love with us both.

A silent, methodical man and not the outgoing, romantic Prince Charming type, he gave my mother and me stability and a good home. My dad stood about five foot nine with thick, brown wavy hair that turned gray by the time he was thirty-five. I never heard him speak of his war experiences until after I was married, when I asked him point blank. By the time I was curious enough to ask, I had finally studied the Korean War in preparation for teaching history. He couldn't say too much before he started to cry. My dad never cried.

He worked two jobs so we could have a nice house and go all out for his latest hobby. Over the course of my years at home it was model airplanes, drag racing, fishing, hunting, water skiing, scuba diving, or motorcycle riding.

I now had a steady home, two parents who loved me, but no idea about any spiritual or inner strength to hold me steady during the turbulent years of the 1960s. If someone had asked me if I believed in God, I would have answered yes, even though I didn't really have a clue about anything having to do with God. I don't remember ever hearing the word *salvation* growing up. I had seen the word *repent* only in a cartoon, which showed a man who looked like Father Time holding a sign that said, "Repent." There was something about the end of the world too, but all I can remember of the messages at church when we did go was that you were supposed to be a "good" person—whatever that meant.

I skipped second grade. I can remember in first grade I wrote a story the teacher read in class. The teachers and administrators must have had a meeting about me, and the next thing I knew I went into third grade instead of second. It made me a year younger than everyone else in my class when I went to high school. I developed physically at an early age, so I had the body of a sixteen-year-old when I was thirteen. My boyfriend, who was a senior when I was a freshman, graduated from high school and went to Vietnam. My neighbor in the same graduating class died there.

Because I was smart, cute, and outgoing, I also developed the idea that I could date any boy, have anything I really wanted, and that somehow I would always come out on top. I loved school and was a cheerleader, homecoming princess, in the school plays, and in all the other activities around school.

My parents were my cheerleaders and told me, "You can grow up and be anything if you work hard for it." Perhaps through me they were living the life they had wished for when they were young. My dad had been sent off to military school as a teen and my mom's family had been desperately poor.

In my memory there stands out only one experience with a church and a pastor making an impression on me. About the time I was in third grade, my parents were having marital problems. I didn't think of it that way until later. They were having talks with a Methodist pastor named Rev. Scott. Everyone called him "Scotty." I don't remember too much about him other than that he was the first and only pastor to be in our home while I was growing up. I remember an ice-cream-making party where there were several ice-cream churns with manual turning handles. The party took place in our upstairs apartment, which was a first. People took turns rotating the handles, and wonderful homemade ice cream appeared. Laughter and fun in a church meeting left an impression on my young mind. Also, when we met for Sunday School singing in the upstairs of the church, Pastor Scotty came up and sang with us. "Deep and wide, deep and wide / There's a fountain flowing deep and wide."

Someday in heaven I hope to let Scotty know how his faithfulness paid off.

In sixth grade we moved to Fremont, California. General Motors had built a huge vehicle factory that hired my dad for an assembly line job. Living in Fremont seemed idyllic. We played softball with the neighborhood kids, rode bikes with other families, and had neighborhood parties and events together. I don't ever remember being afraid when we were out after dark playing hide-and-seek or some other game.

In junior high school I met my best friend, Valerie. After graduating from eighth grade, we went on to Irvington High School together. Her parents were religious and attended the Church of Christ. The main thing I remember about their religion was that they didn't believe in dancing. Valerie's mom was sweet, but her dad was mean. She would sneak out with me and go to dances at the VFW or at school. They were a musical family so I couldn't figure out why they didn't love to dance.

Folk music sung by Peter, Paul, and Mary, Bob Dylan, and Joan Baez was popular at this time. Even though Valerie's family didn't have musical instruments in church, they were allowed to play their guitars, banjos, mandolins, and harpsichords at home. Valerie and I started singing folk songs, playing guitars together, and even sang at a coffee shop together in Hayward. It was there we met our first long-haired older boy. She wanted to know this "older man" of about eighteen with long hair and a beard. It was "cool" and exciting, and we wanted to be hip. I tagged along while she flirted and met with this guy. We kept going to school and being involved in all the extracurricular activities, but we were changing. I discovered that girls were two-faced and couldn't be trusted, and teenage boys were interested mainly in sex. I didn't really understand exactly what it meant either, but the boys kept trying to teach me.

Drive-in movies were the make-out places where sometimes very little movie-watching took place. One poor boy made the mistake of taking me to the movie *Bambi*. I cried so hard when Bambi's mother was shot that there was no make-out time. Poor guy!

By the time I reached twelfth grade, Valerie and I had drifted apart. The truth is that we were both confused and hurt. I became a little bit of a rebel and started hanging out with people who wanted to go to San Francisco to Haight-Ashbury and dance at the Avalon or the Fillmore auditorium. The hippie scene was in full swing by then. As I was trying desperately to grow up, the San Francisco scene looked exciting and a bit dangerous. During my last year of high school through my exposure to hippie ideas, I became aware that the silliness of the high school popularity drama was nonsense, and I didn't want to play that game. I began dating boys who were living on the fringe and were unacceptable to adults.

The idea of being free and throwing off the dictates of society all seemed so romantic. Being on Haight Street and seeing the Grateful Dead having a spontaneous rock concert out of their second-floor apartment seemed wonderful. The laughter, sunshine, and hype of the day were infectious. Janis Joplin screeching out music in Golden Gate Park, and Jefferson Airplane, Country Joe and the Fish, and Paul Revere and the Raiders seemed as if they were telling my story. I caught the dream.

A dream with no substance, a dandelion in the wind—unknown consequences waited for me. Free love wasn't free after all, paying off with pain and confusion. Of course, as a seventeen-year-old I was naive. My mom and dad didn't know how to help me. They thought I was having sex and trying drugs, but not yet, not until after graduation. I was just walking as close to the cliff as was possible without falling over.

2

OVER THE CLIFF

I managed somehow to be a good student and to keep my grades up enough to graduate with honors and get accepted into San Jose State University. In 1967, at seventeen, I wanted to be free from my parents and make all my own decisions.

Really just a foolish little girl who thought that she could do anything, I couldn't wait to move out and go to college. I had been accepted in a new honors humanities program. A group of college professors were trying an experiment in education in which the general education classes would be taken in a block. Students in the experimental program, called "tutorials," could choose their own professors and classes. Instead of the separate general education courses, the classes were taught in sections in which knowledge and learning thoughts overlapped. A retreat weekend to get to know the other students and to interview the professors helped us to decide on the professors we wanted.

The tutorials had their own building, where students could hang out, take classes, and meet with professors for conversations intellectual and otherwise. This school within a school gave students a place to belong. I didn't realize that the humanities department was filled with political radicals. My first experiences with students who were doing drugs, talking anti-war and anti-government, made me feel grown up. I started going to Students for a Democratic Society (SDS) Meetings. SDS, a groupthink code for "communist," had lengthy political discussions. When the conversation turned to revolution and guns, I got spooked and didn't go back.

College became a time of questioning everything. Since I had no God, my life was mainly directed at trying to find truth and to identify what was important. I loved the expanding mental knowledge and the class conversations. The students were thinkers, and the professors were engaged. The combination of being away from home, meeting new people, and exploring exotic new ideas left me stimulated but lost and confused.

Enter Steve—my future husband. When the fall semester of 1967 was about to begin, I answered an ad in the newspaper advertising for a roommate in San Jose near the college. The day I moved in with Marsha, she had picked up a couple of hitchhikers. One of these guys had met Steve in Phoenix, and they had come to California to find him.

Their story about Steve went something like this: Steve and his friend Mike planned to hitchhike to Africa. Of course, this makes no sense. In their mostly stoned-out minds, they would hitchhike to the East Coast, where the plan was to hop a freighter. Thy would get off the boat someplace in Africa where the drugs were cheap, take as many as possible, and go out in a flash.

They made it to Texas. Texans didn't care much for hippies. One night while they were on the road, the driver of a semi tried to run them over and turned around to come back for another try. During their Texas visit Steve and Mike met the guys now looking for them. That would have been before Mike got arrested and Steve called his mom for a bus ticket home.

With the new experience of living away from home, moving in with a roommate, and two strange men showing up, things were exciting. The search for Steve was on. We all decided to try finding this unknown guy named Steve. He had grown up in a town called Saratoga and they had the name of a guy there who might know where Steve was now. They located Barry, a friend of Steve, and found out that Steve was living on his father's property in the Santa Cruz Mountains. After getting general directions, we jumped into Marsha's Karmann Ghia and drove to the mountains.

I'm not exactly sure how we found him, but we did. He had thrown away all his clocks and was trying to find peace through smoking pot and leaving all the stress of life to the city folks. As we sat in the woods next to the creek, it seemed like some peaceful "other world." We all needed some peace.

Sitting by the fire in the middle of a forest, we talked for hours. Steve had just been bailed out of jail by his dad. His long curls and bushy beard had been sheared to present himself to the judge as a reformed man. It all made a great storytelling opportunity around the fire. The case had eventually been thrown out. The jail time in Steve's life was just another exciting story to retell. He wasn't sorry for being at a pot party, just sorry that he had been caught holding the pipe.

The more we talked the more interesting he became. He wasn't too impressed with me. It bothered me because I was not used to being ignored. As I was always up for a challenge, living in a tent trying to get back to nature seemed like the sensible thing to do. I dropped out of school after one semester to go live in the mountains with Steve. At that time I experimented with marijuana and LSD with Steve in the woods, and we did the hippie thing living off the land (sort of) by cooking over a fire and taking baths in the stream. There's was pride in the fact that we were mountain hippies and not city hippies.

In the meantime my folks were flipping out and told me that I was underage and that they were going to call the police on Steve. So, of course, our solution was to go to Reno and get married.

How could a seventeen-year-old get a marriage license? I had a driver's license that said I was eighteen because my parents had lied to get me my driver's license early. Steve was eighteen so his dad had to send him permission to get married. The legal age for a marriage license was eighteen for women and twenty-one for men.

A friend of Steve's drove us to Reno. We didn't really know the people we stayed with while we were waiting for Steve's dad to mail his permission letter. A romantic blur, we expected to drive up one day and come back the next. Every good character in a fairy tale must overcome difficulties to find true love. Standing in the court office before Judge Beamer, in clothes that we had worn for two days, I was married in bright-orange velvet pants. The judge's somber words at the end of the ceremony were—"Good luck," which he obviously believed we needed.

Raised reading fairy tales, I just knew that we would live happily ever after. At that time the Beatles sang a song called "The Fool on the Hill." To me, Steve was "the fool on the hill" the Beatles sang about. He was a quiet, meditative kind of person from a very intellectual but dysfunctional family. With few people skills, no happy family memories, no father figure who taught him anything, he was clueless when it came to relationships.

I was a silly girl with big dreams. After we got married, the reality of things like a job, a place to live, and making decisions together became the ongoing saga—which didn't go very smoothly. I had no idea what love was and had married someone I didn't know. Caught on the playground merry-go-round of life, I couldn't get off, and "the eyes in my head could see the world spinning around," as the song lyrics suggested.

3

GLORY HILL AND SALVATION

After we were married, we did odd jobs, knitted scarves to sell, rented places to live, and generally bumped around. When it began raining, the tent in the forest didn't seem as romantic. The latest in the series of apartments was in Los Gatos, California. That particular apartment was memorable for two reasons: (1) the landlady was a crab, and (2) I read the *Hobbit* and the *Lord of the Rings* trilogy in the same week. Steve told me later that one night while sleeping I sat straight up in bed and yelled, "There's trouble in Mordor!" and lay straight back down on the bed. We lived in an upstairs apartment over the landlady's apartment. That meant that she could hear every time we made noise or walked or ran around the apartment.

We decided we needed a new apartment and wanted to live in the woods, but not in a tent. Looking for places to hang out with people like us, we went into the local "head shop." A head shop sold beads, tie-dye clothes, and smoking paraphernalia.

We talked with a couple in the shop and told them that we were looking for a place to rent in the Santa Cruz Mountains. It turned out that they had just moved out of a cabin and it might still be for rent.

"The landlords are a little strange. They're religious but they're nice," they told us.

With directions in hand, the next day I drove up to look at the cabin. I dressed up (in my opinion) for the occasion. Getting out of the car in a very short miniskirt, tights, and knee-length boots, I was greeted by two Australian shepherd dogs and a lady with a big smile.

Beverly Walrath was thirty-six at this time. In my eyes she was an older, motherly looking lady. With her long hair up in a funny-looking roll on her head, no make-up or jewelry, and a mid-calf dress, she looked safe in an Amish kind of way.

We talked while sitting at the table in a kitchen of a place that would later be referred to as "Glory Hill." The kitchen was spotless and smelled like home cooking. I remember today the safe and peaceful feeling of that first conversation. I don't remember what we talked about, only that I came away hopeful. She showed me the small cabin not far from the main house. With a kitchen, bedroom, and a bathroom for seventy-five dollars a month, it seemed perfect.

When I left her that day, I was encouraged by the prospect of renting the cabin. Beverly wanted to first talk it over with her husband, Wally. Later she recounted her first impression of me that she shared to Wally. They were new Christians themselves, and Beverly prayed and wanted to share her faith. Since

I had shown up in my best miniskirt, boots, and hippie-type clothing, she knew that I had made an effort. She did some tall talking to her husband. Wally, the practical one, wasn't sure about taking on two mixed-up kids. We still looked like the hippies we were, but they took a chance on us. We were thrilled with the small cabin and gathered up our few possessions to move in as quickly as we could.

The idea of living on a mini-farm fit in with our back-to-nature ideal. Of course, we knew absolutely zero about farm animals or growing food. One Sunday morning I planned to make French toast for breakfast and discovered that we were out of milk. When I told Steve we couldn't have French toast because we were out of milk, he sagely suggested, "Why don't you go up and get some milk from one of the goats?"

Thinking it was a great solution, I grabbed a cup and headed for the goat barn. I could do this. I had seen Beverly milk the goat—once.

The goat barn was up the hill close to the cabin. After confidently walking to the barn, I carefully put the goat into the milking stall and placed my little cup under her. Sitting on the milking stool, I felt like a real farm girl. Perched nearby, the cat anxiously awaited her portion. I began diligently yanking on the goat and to my dismay, no milk came out. Nanny turned to look at me with her big questioning eyes. I yanked on her for some time before giving up. I never got milk and I wasn't kicked. Later Beverly showed me how to find success when milking a goat.

As time went on, Steve and I were smoking pot and aimlessly living each day.

Life at this time was bumpy and we barely existed. Jobs were not important, and I don't remember how we came up with money for rent and food.

Wally and Beverly were praying for us, I now know that we were now their mission field. The couple had recently become Christians as God had used Beverly's children to reach her heart. The local Free Methodists held a children's camp every year. Beverly had two sons from a previous marriage and was trying to be a good mother, so she dropped the boys off each day for the camp.

One day she stood in the back for the end of the service. The evangelist had an altar call in which he invited the boys and girls to come forward to pray if they did not have Jesus in their hearts. She heard enough of the gospel message to come to the awareness that she needed God herself. A few days later she knelt at the couch in her front room and found God.

Marley Walrath, better known as "Wally," worked for a company in Palo Alto and commuted an hour each way to work every day. Wally was fifteen years older than Beverly. He would sing a little song to her that went something like "I'd rather be an old man's sweetheart than a young man's slave."

Not long after Beverly's experience with God, Wally followed in Beverly's footsteps and became a believer. His non-Christian habits were harder to break away from because he had been an unbeliever for many years. He used to say, "This house [meaning himself] may not look like much now—but you should have seen it before!"

Steve and I noticed they were always off to church on Sunday mornings. During the week on Wednesday nights I would hear singing coming from the house. I finally asked Beverly about the music. She they told me they got together with friends and sang and read the Bible together. The music was church music, but I have always loved music and singing so I was curious.

Finally we went to one of their singing and Bible-reading times. It seemed like a good thing to do. We knew absolutely nothing about what it meant to be a Christian. We started asking questions and spending more time with them. They were very loving and somewhat adopted us. We went to church with them and made our first attempts at Christianity. The crossroads came when I looked at their church rule book.

There were more rules than I had ever seen. The church manual spelled out what to do and not do, wear and not wear, and a list of places where Christians shouldn't go. Even though these people had offered us love and community, I was not ready to follow the rules. Plus, Steve and I were fighting. He thought I was uptight and pushy, and I thought he was a lazy pig.

I was a little girl playing house, and the marriage thing, which at first seemed like the thing to do, started looking like not the best idea that I had ever thought of. Steve spent most of the time lying around, a little boy in a man's body. He had no drive, no ambition, and just wanted to play.

The dreams that I had imagined about marriage didn't resemble my reality. There was no Prince Charming to sweep me off my feet, fight my battles, and treat me like a princess.

We moved out and went to another cabin in the woods, but life wasn't better. We were too selfish, immature, and lost.

Then I went home to my parents.

4

SURRENDER

My parents welcomed me with open arms. They had little faith in the durability of our marriage. They didn't like Steve and were glad to have me back home. Now I would be finished with this hippie experiment and be like them again. I enrolled at Ohlone Community College but didn't finish the semester. I started not caring. I dated guys I thought my parents would like and some I knew they wouldn't. Feeling guilty for disappointing my parents, I tried fitting back into their lifestyle but couldn't do it. Something had changed. I was no longer the fun-loving daughter they once knew. It just didn't work.

After a few months I decided to find out where Steve had gone after we separated. Someone told me he had gone to see his sister in Beaver, Oregon. Deciding to find out for myself, I got money together to fly part of the way. When I ran out of cash, I started hitchhiking. Nearing dark, I found myself on the side of the road with my thumb out on a deserted coastal road in Oregon.

At this time in life I wasn't afraid of anything. I had a combination of super-idealism and youthful stupidity. Realizing I only "sort of" knew the directions to Steve's sister's house, I didn't get scared until later. There I stood on a mostly deserted road looking for a ride. I had on wool pants from a military surplus store, a coat, and a snow beanie. Holding my guitar case and backpack, I stuck out my thumb and wondered if I would get a ride or have to walk all the way. Finally in the dark a single car stopped.

A large middle-aged man sat behind the wheel. I couldn't see him very well, but I jumped in just the same. I wouldn't have to walk. I remember he asked me all kinds of questions. He asked what I would do if someone propositioned me, and I politely told him I was a married woman and would say no. Still very naive, I just answered and told him my life story—my husband, Steve, and I were currently separated, and I thought he might be visiting his sister in Beaver. I was on my way to find my husband.

God looked out for me even in my ignorance. The man ended up taking me right to my sister-in-law's doorstep. I suppose there were not too many hippies living in Beaver, so he knew right where to go. Not too long after this, a girl got her arms chopped off and raped in the same area. *Then* I got scared.

I never hitchhiked again.

Arriving at Steve's sister's house in the middle of the night didn't matter. I found Steve's brother's girlfriend, Mary Ann, staying with her. The next day she told me that Steve and his older brother, Larry, had left to drive to Alaska. Steve's sister, Susan, and their brother, Larry, didn't like me much. They said I reminded them of their mother, whom they didn't like much either. They were happy to tell me that Steve had ripped up our marriage license and had moved on with his life. From this point on I thought I would never see him again.

I got a ride with a friend who took me into Portland, Oregon, where I met people there who gave me a place to live. I started looking for employment and took odd jobs to get by. The time in Portland, a dark time in my life, found me more lost and confused. I didn't fit in anywhere. I worked various jobs and lived with a group of hippies who rented rooms in a two-story, run-down house in a slummy part of town.

One day as I walked aimlessly around town, I stopped and realized I was standing in front of a church. It must have been a Sunday morning because I remember feeling so alone—and there were people singing. I don't remember the song, but the hymn came across loud and clear. With no emotional energy to face anyone and with little hope, I stood and listened. God tried helping me, but I felt too lost, too hopeless. After listening in despair for a few minutes, I walked on. The people in the little church never knew a lost and lonely girl had stood outside and listened to their singing.

As time went on, things didn't improve. From Portland I went to look at a commune with the current man in my life. The farm and surrounding countryside were beautiful, but the people were weird—even to me. They seemed listless and lazy, so we didn't stay. Finally we ended up in Seattle. There we were offered a job taking tickets at a rock festival outside Seattle. It seemed that it would be great fun. The Hell's Angels had also been hired to oversee security. Maybe I would meet some of the band people and musicians. I met some people all right, but not who I expected.

The day came and we drove outside Seattle to the land where the festival would take place. I checked in and began taking tickets at the gate. At that time a group of people who looked like everyone else coming to the festival sat down by the entry gate. A group of them were talking with people and passing out papers. A smiling girl walked right up to me and said, "Jesus is coming again soon, sister. Are you ready?"

Obviously I knew I wasn't ready for anything. They sang and played guitars and talked about how their lives had been changed through salvation in Jesus. They called themselves "Jesus freaks." I listened to what they had to say. They seemed harmless and looked just like me. Before they left, someone gave me the address in Seattle where they lived together in a house full of Christians.

After the festival I went back to Seattle. It was an unhappy period, hanging out with people who were messed up—when I finally remembered the Jesus freaks. I found the address they had given me and decided to leave my current living situation and go find them. They looked like hippies and didn't have a rule book—this must be a better answer. My showing up at their door didn't surprise them. When I told them I had been given the address at the rock festival, they welcomed me inside. Immediately they began asking me questions about my salvation.

"Where are you with Jesus?" they asked.

I was nowhere. Before I knew it, I was kneeling with a group who were praying for me to become a Christian. I told Jesus right then that I wanted to be a real Christian and would follow Him.

Since I didn't have a place to live and the house was full, they suggested I get a ride to another place with a girl they knew who would be driving up to a commune near the Washington-Canadian border. Living with a group of Christians in a communal style appealed to my need to belong and be accepted. The Bible talks about the early Christians sharing all things and living together after Pentecost. It seemed to be part of learning to live as the Bible Christians lived.

Life at the commune did not turn out to be the utopia I had imagined, however. There were no drugs and the people prayed, but they lacked leadership, and every person went his or her own way to figure things out. I didn't give up. Still trying to follow Jesus but not exactly sure how to do it, I struggled on. I wondered about Steve. Would I ever see him again?

Steve, I found out later, worked on a firefighting crew in Alaska for about six months. The forestry department supplied room and board. The room meant three meals a day—military rations, C rations left over from the Korea Conflict—and the housing was a piece of plastic and a rope to make a tent. They dropped the crew out in the middle of nowhere to dig ditches for fire breaks.

As a baby Christian I had questions, and the group didn't have many answers. They loved God but needed a shepherd. God was still watching over me and had gone to great lengths to help me to get my life back on track. I still remembered Wally's and Beverly's names because they were the first people to talk to me about the Bible and faith in Jesus.

After I had been at the commune for a month, a new couple showed up. One day we talked and shared our previous lives. I told them about the first people who taught me about salvation, the story of the rock festival, and how I ended up at the commune.

"Far out!" the husband said. While they were hitchhiking through California, some guy had given them a ride and the address and phone number of a Christian couple he knew in Santa Cruz, California. They found the piece of paper with the address of Beverly and Wally in the Santa Cruz Mountains. What are the odds of someone showing up at the Washington-Canadian border, where about thirty Jesus people lived, who would hand me Wally and Beverly's address?

I called them the next day to tell them what had happened in my life. They had been praying for Steve and me often, I guess. They asked me to come back and stay at their house. I got on a plane with another girl, Elaine, who just happened to have relatives not far from Santa Cruz. She had been a witch and into the occult before becoming a Christian. She offered to pay for my plane fare, and we were off to the next adventure. This time Jesus went with me. When I showed up at Wally and Beverly's house, they welcomed me like the prodigal daughter.

They had heard from Steve the previous week. He had sent them a letter with a check in it to help build a church. We did not know it at the time but God was working in both of our lives.

In Alaska Steve had prayed and promised the Lord he would send Wally and Beverly a tithe of his money from his work if he got a job. He kept his promise. From the check they figured he might be back in California. Beverly went to the bank the check came from, and they told her Steve might be on his dad's property in the Santa Cruz Mountains. Since Steve had grown up in Saratoga, the bank personnel knew his family. We decided we would try to find him.

Beverly and I went up to the mountains to look for Steve. I knew the general direction to find his dad's property. On the dirt road we saw a sign with an arrow that said "Steve and Judy." Thinking for sure that Steve had a girl with him named Judy, I dreaded what we might find. The idea of seeing Steve with a new girlfriend scrambled my emotions.

"Judy" turned out to be a dog.

We found Steve living in a cabin his brother had built. Beverly went up to him and shook the sleeping bag he was lying in. "Steven," she said, "how are you doing in your soul?"

When Steve looked up and saw Beverly, he covered his head and said, "*Oh, no!*"

Beverly gave Steve and me a chance to be alone. In an awkward conversation, Steve and I talked about what we had both been doing. It wasn't a pretty picture for either of us. We had always been honest with each other, so it became a time of confession. I recounted all the wrong things I had been involved in while we were apart and told him about my experience of getting saved and becoming a serious follower of Jesus. He confessed all the wrong things that he had been involved in as well. I knew I couldn't stay with Steve in the cabin. Being so close to the old life would not be healthy for me spiritually.

"If I'm going to really live for God, I need to stay with Wally and Beverly at their house. Would you like to try again and give Jesus and our marriage another chance?" I asked.

"I don't want to be talked into anything. If God is real, I need to know it for myself," he replied.

Steve didn't want to go back to Wally and Beverly's house. I went back there and Steve decided to go to Yosemite. I'm not sure why he chose Yosemite, but my guess is that he wanted to get away from any influences that might get in the way of his finding God for himself. He wanted to pray and see if what they were saying turned out to be a mind game or something else.

Gone for three days, he prayed—and *we* prayed. Alone at a campsite with his own thoughts, he asked God to be real to him. He slept outside, prayed, and read the Bible. For hours he wrestled with his doubt and unbelief. In the night he had nightmares and felt things tugging at the foot of his sleeping bag. The time came when he knew. One day he drove up the driveway and announced that he knew he had met the Lord. "Guess who found Jesus!" he yelled out the car window. Ready to give it another try, he moved back with me to Glory Hill.

In just a few years God would keep sending this very straight-laced couple young people who were hungry to know about God and a Jesus who loved and died so they could be changed.

God is real and is always ready to teach us how to live.

5

GROWING UP IN JESUS

In the time after Steve and I became Christians, we were mostly trying to grow up. Steve wanted to get a job, I learned how to cook something besides bread and cake, and our first baby on the way gave us a crash course. My parents were horrified. I had gone from one extreme to another. My mother told me, "You don't have to make yourself ugly to be a Christian."

We lived at Glory Hill for a month or two, but the house got crowded and we needed a place of our own since we had taken in several girls and boys who had been recently saved to get them off the streets.

Family meals and devotions were nightly events. We gathered for church services in the front room. The couches and chairs were removed and carried to the deck. Folding chairs were put in place with a small pulpit in front of the fireplace, facing the chairs. The front room became so crowded that the person playing the piano had to stay at the piano after finishing until the end of the service.

When we moved out of the cabin it was time to call a pastor. Rev. John Miller and his wife, Juanita, accepted the call. They were the sweetest people. Coming from the Midwest and being raised in the church gave them no preparation for what they found in Santa Cruz. They prayed, preached, and lived the Christian life in front of the unusual congregation they served. Pastor Miller was a tall man. When he preached and moved around much, he had to be careful not to bump his head on the low ceiling in the front room. He learned how to contain his natural excitement while being cautious!

Glory Hill gave us such a sense of belonging. Life took on routines, but we were clueless about a multitude of things. Wally went to work every day, so Beverly handled the training. To learn how to live a Christian-based life, the girls were being taught to cook, can food, and sew. The boys were made to do chores around the house and look for work when they were ready. Like most of the residents, Steve and I were raised in suburbia, where all food came from the grocery store. We learned a little about gardening and preserving food. This all seemed like great fun to return to nature. However, we soon found out that gardening required a lot of hard work.

One day Steve came home from looking for work. Really discouraged, he had left the employment office after finding that the only job he qualified for was one that involved picking brussels sprouts. Being a farm worker didn't appeal to him and he looked at it as beneath his dignity. Somewhere between the time he rejected brussels-sprout-picking and getting home, he decided that God had called him to preach.

Beverly and I were sitting in the kitchen when he came home and announced, "The Lord is calling me to preach."

"Oh, really?" Beverly said.

Her skepticism came because many of the young people thought being called to preach meant you didn't have to work. Not known for his great work ethic, after time Steve got a job, engaged in some earnest prayer, added a little growing up, and decided he really did have a call to ministry—and it was not just because he didn't want to pick brussels sprouts!

Steve got a job at a furniture-making company and went to work every day. We found a house to rent in Scotts Valley, an old chinchilla hut converted into a cabin. As baby Christians, we weren't too far away from the old way of thinking. The dignity factor was missing for sure.

For example, Wally and Beverly were horrified when I showed up at one prayer meeting riding Steve's Honda 90. As I drove up the highway from Scotts Valley to the Walraths' house, a trucker honked his horn and waved at me as I rode the motorbike up the mountain road to Glory Hill. I probably did look funny in my long dress, my hair in a bun, and by now six months pregnant. No dignity here—I obviously had some major growing-up to do.

By the time our first son, Matthew, was born, we had upgraded to a real cabin with a wood stove, kitchen, and bedroom. Before we moved to the larger cabin, Steve had some work to do in our recent cabin. Not wanting to go out for wood for the stove when it rained, he had built a huge box in the corner of the front room to put wood in. He had to tear it into pieces before we emptied the cabin because it wouldn't fit through the front door.

At Glory Hill the front room was no longer adequate to hold everyone for our church meetings. Wally built a shed with a chemical toilet and had boys in bunks in other sheds. Wally, Beverly, and the new pastor, John Miller, searched for a larger place to hold services. They found an old church building in downtown Santa Cruz, on Elm Street, with an unused sanctuary. The back rooms of the church housed the painters' and plumbers' union. It had originally been the First Advent Christian Church. When the church congregation dwindled, they had rented out the back rooms to the painters' and plumbers' unions for offices. The sanctuary part stood empty. By faith the church rented the front of the building. Painters and plumbers didn't need it on Sundays, so the front of the building, the sanctuary, was subleased to the church.

The inside of the church had high ceilings, wood paneling, and stained-glass windows. Built at the turn of the century, it was a substantial church structure, standing like a sentinel just off the main street of Santa Cruz. It had seen tremendous changes in the town of Santa Cruz. Street upgrades found buried pipes made of redwood trees still in the ground. The downtown now had shops and eating places, and "The Catalyst," a large bar and dance hall where live bands like the Beach Boys and Janis Joplin performed. It drew all kinds of interesting people to town. At this time it was located right across the street from the church on Elm Street. Fortunately, the loud amplified rock music didn't blast on Sunday mornings—the all-night partygoers would be crashed out sleeping by then.

We tried to put every leased inch to good use. A narrow set of stairs led to an upper room, which served as an office at one time. This small beginning turned into Elm Street Mission and served the homeless and hippies of Santa Cruz. The first sack lunches with peanut-butter-and-jelly sandwiches were assembled there and passed out from the back of a station wagon. In later years, after the hippie era, full meals were cooked and served. The mission is still in operation after fifty years. The people have changed, but it is still there to tell the gospel story.

Glory Hill now had people sleeping in every nook and cranny. Wally and Beverly met Grace Jones, who had property in Hesperia and a ministry called "The Desert Lighthouse." Grace's ministry with her husband was directly primarily to prisoners and drug addicts. Her husband died and she tried keeping the ministry going, but without him it wasn't very successful. The decision to combine ministries and assets made it possible for the Walraths to sell Glory Hill and Grace's property and purchase a large property in Santa Cruz on El Rancho Drive. What became known as the "Shepherd's Fold" had served as a hotel and wayside dancehall in the 1920s, originally called the Tower Lodge Inn. During the Prohibition time they probably served more than lemonade. It had ten bedrooms, two kitchens, eight living rooms counting the small cabins and houses on the property, and a ballroom that was extended out the back on huge redwood pilings. It was a two-and-a-half-acre piece of land selling for $65,000 at the time.

The upstairs had a living room, dining area, and kitchen. On the downstairs level another kitchen, more rooms, and a ballroom with a hardwood floor made the property perfect. The downstairs rooms became the sewing room, the canning kitchen, and storage area. With plenty of room available for expansion and housing the hippies who kept showing up, it seemed perfect. Young men and women now had a place to get off the streets, find Jesus, and begin new lives.

An example of how God takes trials and turns them into blessings came not long after the Walraths sold their property and moved from Glory Hill to the Shepherd's Fold. In December 1974 they moved to the new property. In February, just two months later, Beverly woke up to choking smoke. Wally called the fire department and found flames in the downstairs kitchen. The fire department was able to put out the fire caused by faulty wiring, and the damage was mainly in the downstairs kitchen area.

There was one wall in the whole property that had fire-retardant materials put up—the wall that separated the kitchen from the ballroom. The firemen told Wally that if that wall had not been there and if the fire had reached the ballroom area, the whole place would have gone up in flames. It became known as "the wall that saved it all."

"How could this happen?" I'm sure they asked. Later, the insurance money from the fire damage paid for the new wiring and bringing the area up to code. They would never have been able to obtain a use permit if those renovations bringing it up to the fire code had not been made.

The ministry moved into the large home and church building downtown. The group now had the building and

tools to do God's work in Santa Cruz. In the middle of all
of this, as the first hippies sent to the Walraths, we were now
the old-timers and ready for the next step. Several ministers
and evangelists came by the Santa Cruz church to be a part of
God's work. One of these men, an evangelist named J. E. Ray,
a pastor from Davenport, Iowa, visited the church and took an
interest in Steve and me.

Hearing Steve had a call to the ministry, Pastor Ray
talked to us about a Bible college in Rock Island, Illinois. It
educated future ministers in the Bible Missionary Church,
a small denomination. Recently widowed, he owned a large
two-story house where he lived alone. His home and church
in Davenport were just across the river from the Bible college,
located in Rock Island, Illinois. Pastor Ray offered to rent us
an affordable room in his house while Steve studied for the
ministry if we wanted to come to the Bible college.

Wally and Beverly weren't overly excited about our moving
to Iowa. They were familiar with some of the very strict rules
of the church we were all affiliated with, the Bible Missionary
Church. The Bible college, as the mecca of the denomination
and bastion of theological purity and conservatism, was a place
they were afraid for us to go because we might not easily handle
the change and even stricter rules than we were accustomed to.
Despite their voiced reservations, we decided we should go.

A call to preach is a call to prepare.

6

OFF TO BIBLE SCHOOL

"Iowa or bust" became our motto. Today it would take the largest U-Haul to move our possessions. But back then we were able to load all our earthly possessions into our white 1959 Ford. We put our one-year-old baby, Matthew, on top of the pile in the back seat and set off. We dubbed our car "the ark" because over the years we made numerous trips across the country, back and forth between California and Iowa, and it just kept floating along.

At the Bible college we were treated like a cross between special people and freaks of nature. Everyone wanted to hear our testimonies about all the different kinds of outrageous sins we had experienced. We didn't want to talk about our previous lifestyle of sin, only the salvation part of our testimony. Steve gave his testimony in a Spanish-speaking church in Chicago, and the flyer said something like "Come and hear Steve Palm, who injected continuously . . ." Since it was written in Spanish, we didn't read the translation until after we arrived at the church. Neither of us had ever tried hard drugs and certainly never injected anything.

We found the students at the Bible college very young and sheltered. Some didn't think they had an exciting testimony, but I always felt thankful they hadn't experienced the scars of sin we carried.

I could often gauge how the Bible school girls were doing spiritually. When they were praying and doing well, they all wanted to be my friend. When they weren't doing so well, they avoided me. I took a few classes at a local community college, and some of my fellow students became Christians.

One day a boy of about twelve knocked at our front door. "I'm selling engraved Social Security cards. Would you like to buy one?" he asked. I invited him in and sat down with him as Beverly had once done with me. Over cookies and milk, the boy, named Dennis, told me his story. His father was an alcoholic and in jail. His mother was bedridden most of the time. He tried selling things door to door to make a little extra money and mostly took care of himself. Steve and I tried to help Dennis and invited him to church. He came back from time to time to visit us and occasionally would come to church. During the time at the Bible college, Steve and I were always involved in evangelism, and the lives of some of the people we met there have been lasting relationships.

Our first Christmas in Iowa was now one that we look back on as one of the best. We bought an eight-foot tree and took it home in our car with it laid across the back seat and part of it sticking out an open window. I hadn't considered that we didn't have anything to put on it for decorations. Because I was a stay-at-home mom, I had the time to be creative, so I baked Christmas ornaments and painted them. The boys and I made long paper ropes. We popped popcorn and with a needle and thread strung the kernels together to make more ropes to wind around the tree. To us it was the most beautiful tree we had ever had. Steve put a flat square package under the tree. My only present looked to me as if he had bought me a pair of nylons. I knew we were poor, so I tried not to feel bad toward him for such a horrible (but useful) present. To my total shock, when I opened the gift I found myself looking at a booklet of sewing machine directions. Steve had arranged to pay ten dollars a month to buy me my first sewing machine.

During our time at the Bible college Steve and I got a letter from his brother, Larry. When we were first exposed to Christians, Larry had cautioned Steve to stay away from them. "They'll try to convert you," he warned. We didn't stay away from the Christians, of course, and the gap between Steve and Larry became huge. Larry lived with his girlfriend in the mountains, smoking dope and living the hippie lifestyle, and according to him we had become ultra-conservative Bible-thumpers. We looked at Larry as a lost cause and had almost no faith that he would ever get saved.

In the letter we received from Larry, he wrote to us about an experience he had. After we had left for Bible college, Larry thought of a plan. He knew the Walraths loved to try getting people saved. Wally and Beverly stayed in contact with Larry after we left. He learned enough about what he considered a game and knew a little about what made these crazy Christians happy. He planned to steal Wally's car. He thought that if he went to the altar at church and acted as if he wanted religion, they would trust him, and his theft would be easier to pull off. At the end of the service he went to the altar to pray. But something strange happened. Larry started praying in earnest, and He met Jesus—instead of stealing a car.

At Bible college we met and listened to some of the best Christian ministers and finest people. The district leader and his wife, Frank and Ann Baldwin, encouraged and cheered us on as we tried fitting into this new culture. I realize today how gracious and welcoming they were, especially when we first arrived. We were still rough around the edges. Aggressive and outgoing, I still slapped men on the back and probably seemed forward and unladylike to these very serious saints. They loved us anyway.

During those four years at the Bible college another member of Steve's family showed up in Iowa to see us, his sister, Susan. She knocked on our door one day with her two small sons, Wesley and Richard. Richard was just a baby, and Wesley was dressed in a home-cured animal skin shirt. Susan was proud of the fact that she had cured the skin in urine herself, but it looked dirty and didn't smell great to me. The baby, outfitted in home-sewn clothes, looked like a frontier baby. Susan was planning to divorce her husband and go to Alaska with the kids for a new start. Being nine months pregnant myself with our second child, I wasn't much excited by company, but I really wanted Susan to find Jesus.

To add to the chaos, Steve had been scheduled to go for the first time before the ministerial board to be interviewed for his district minister's license. I went into labor, Steve went to the meeting, and Susan stayed home with her two boys and our son, Matthew. I had a long labor with Andrew, our second son. As I lay in the hospital, I thought about Susan at home and tried figuring out a way she could hear the gospel. Then I remembered the camp meeting coming up in July. Pastors and people from all over the district came for a week during the summer and had Bible studies, children's meetings, prayer times, and three preaching services a day.

The Iowa-Illinois district campgrounds, located in the country outside Rock Island, had buildings constructed by volunteer labor, including dormitories and a home for the district leader and his family. A funny story told to us by Frank Baldwin, the district leader, went something like this: when they first purchased the property, an overzealous Christian put up a sign with the rules on it at the front gate. One of the rules listed said, "No pants on women." The neighbors thought a nudist colony had moved to the area.

We thought of the camp meeting as a "Jesus party." We ate communally, slept in dorms, prayed around the clock, went to church three times a day, and basically camped out for a week. The services were held in a large circus-style tent. We brought Andrew home from the hospital on one of the first days of the camp meeting. I thought that if we could just get Susan to go to camp, she would get saved. We somehow convinced her to go with us. I'm not sure how our new friends reacted to Susan and her boys, or to me being there with a two-day-old baby. Susan looked and acted like the hippie she was. She did wear long, flowing dresses, as did the other women at the campgrounds, but didn't bother with a blanket or nursing clothing. She shocked men, women, and children with her breastfeeding whenever and wherever. I finally asked her to go to the girls' dorm and try to cover up a little. Even in the dorm the little girls giggled in embarrassment. We found out later that Sister Baldwin had talked to the ladies and quieted their comments and anxieties.

In one of the afternoon services Steve, Susan, her boys, and I sat toward the front of the big tent with Matthew and Andrew. As the evangelist finished the sermon, a huge Illinois rain and windstorm hit the tent. The lights flickered and the wind started pulling out the tent stakes. The sound was deafening. People prayed out loud, the lights went out, and the wind and rain beat against the tent.

The preacher did what preachers do and held an altar call, inviting people to come forward and pray. Sitting next to her on the hard wooden seats, exhausted and weak, I prayed Susan had understood the salvation message. The rain pounded, the wind blew—and Susan went forward to pray.

A retired missionary from India, Billie Holstein, took my new baby and someone else took Matthew, and I went forward to pray with Susan. By then the men were calling for help to hold the tent down. The noise nearly overwhelmed us, deafening between the sound of the rain, the tent flapping, and the men yelling for help. Someone shouted for hammers and stakes to keep the tent from flying away. Susan remembers thinking they needed hammers for her to beat out her frustrations. Despite the chaos, Susan was saved. She finished praying, praised God for His forgiveness, the rain stopped, and the sun came out.

The district leader didn't miss a beat. As we rejoiced in Susan's salvation, he took up an offering to retire the tent and build a new permanent building. Those grounds saw some wonderful miracles of grace take place then and through the years. The days of week-long camp meetings are mostly a time in history now, but it is a part of my spiritual foundation. I am better for living it and having had the privilege of seeing and experiencing the ways God works.

During our time in Iowa and Illinois we saw young people find God, students raised in the church get settled, and we added to our family. A pastor's wife introduced me to a troubled young lady named Faith, whose parents had been killed in a tragic car accident. She had been through too much for such a young person. She was attending the Bible school but not doing well. Of course, my answer was the Shepherd's Fold. I just knew that if I could get her to California, Wally and Beverly would know what to do with her.

I talked her into giving it a try, so Faith and I plus our two small boys, Matthew and Andrew, packed our Volkswagen Bug and headed for California. We made it to just outside Elko, Nevada, and the car broke down. We thought of hitchhiking into town, but two women holding two babies hitchhiking didn't seem like such a good idea. We called Wally, and he contacted a local Nazarene pastor and his wife, and they came and picked us up. Not too many pastors would have wanted to take home two women and two babies who were total strangers. They were kind and gracious and let us stay with them until the Santa Cruz folks could come to our rescue. Faith and I have remained friends through the years, and God did help her.

After almost four years of Bible college, we now had three boys. Born in Davenport, Ben made our family of five complete. I almost didn't make it to the hospital. Steve and a friend were out buying ice cream when I went into labor. A friend insisted on driving us to the hospital because of having a larger car. While we waited for the car, Ben decided he wanted to be born. By the time we made it to the hospital, there were several nurses yelling directions and running down the hall pushing me to the maternity area.

One scare for us came when Steve lost about forty pounds. His six-foot frame looked cadaver-like, and I just knew he had cancer. We had insurance from Steve's job, so I convinced him to make a doctor's appointment.

The doctor ran lab tests and asked Steve a few questions. "How much are you working? How much are you sleeping?" he asked.

Steve told the doctor his schedule—going to Bible school for his classes in the morning, coming home to eat, going to work at the warehouse for eight hours, coming home and sleeping four or five hours Monday through Friday. On the weekends we went to church twice and sometimes held services at rest homes, jails, or had street meetings. He managed a little studying in between.

The doctor chuckled and told him to get some more sleep. He also gave him a steroid shot to increase his appetite. To this day Steve still blames his weight gains on that shot.

During our time in the Iowa-Illinois area we were shown huge amounts of grace by the Christians there. When Steve graduated with his bachelor's in theology, we were expected to go to pastor a church. Those deemed ready to pastor a church were called by various district leaders throughout the United States and asked to pray about serving churches needing a pastor. Of course, our friends in Santa Cruz wanted us to move back to California, but God had other plans.

It was time for a call to our first church.

7

MONMOUTH, ILLINOIS

During the four years at Bible college, Steve had many opportunities to preach at jails, on the streets in Davenport and Rock Island, and the surrounding areas. We filled in for pastors who went on vacation or needed to be away from their churches.

One of the places we filled in was at a little church in Monmouth, Illinois, that had a huge old two-story parsonage, the original farmhouse for the property. The pastor serving there commuted from Rock Island and didn't live in the parsonage. We fell in love with the town and the little church. We thought that if God wanted us to go to Monmouth, He would work it out. We prayed.

Now finished with college and four years older, we had learned many lessons in trusting God. At times during the Bible college years we were so poor that Steve didn't have money for oil, gas, and the ten-cent toll fee on the bridge to get to Bible school, which was the fastest route across the river to get from Davenport to Rock Island. One day running late and headed for this bridge, he realized he didn't have ten cents for the toll. He prayed. Not knowing what else to do, he opened the car door at the toll booth and looked down. There on the pavement a shiny dime waited.

Another time, Steve's car came to a stop as it ran out of oil. To his surprise, along came the pastor and a friend, took oil out of their trunk, put it into Steve's engine, and off he went to his classes. In so many ways God provided. We were certain God would let us know where He wanted us.

The district leader, Brother Baldwin, wanted to keep us around, so he asked us to pray about pastoring at one of three available churches. By the time he mentioned Monmouth, the last on his list, he had about given up, seeming almost embarrassed to ask us about it since there was very little there. He was surprised when we said yes almost immediately.

We were excited and blessed to be considered for any church. God had nudged us, and it worked out that we would be answering the call in Monmouth. Ten people attended the first Sunday, and we were five of them. In 1973 to be offered a place to live, paid utilities, and twenty-five dollars a week seemed too good to be true. We decided to move as soon as possible. Steve could commute to Rock Island for his last class days, and we could get started. On Thanksgiving Day we packed up our three children and our growing number of boxes of our possessions and headed to Monmouth. I had cooked a turkey before we left and put it into the oven—then we loaded the stove, turkey, and everything else into the U-Haul truck.

I'm not sure now if we remembered that the house had been vacant for three years. We were excited about the beautiful old farmhouse with so much room and the old-fashioned fireplace with a cast-iron covering. Not realizing an empty house meant many surrounding animals and insects had moved in, we learned a thing or two. Unloading enough of our possessions to have Thanksgiving dinner, Steve, our three boys, and I had an adventurous day ahead and were in for a few surprises after dinner when we went to work. A very ornate cover was at the opening of the fireplace. Thinking a small fire might be nice, we opened the fireplace. For our first lesson about vacant houses, we found two dried-up, dead squirrels wrapped around the fireplace grate.

There were many mice traveling between the upstairs and downstairs floors—we could hear them running in the ceilings. For days after we moved in, we heard the snapping of mousetraps and the squeals of mice. A cat-size rat lived in the basement. I had never seen a rat. When I first saw him, he looked at me as if he were wondering what I was doing in his basement. They probably heard my scream in the next town.

With the extra "company," we learned our first lessons in insect and varmint extermination. Flypaper, D-con, and mousetraps were reasonable and necessary purchases at our new church.

As a married couple, Steve and I had never lived in a house so big. There were two staircases, a dining room, a sitting room, a kitchen and living room downstairs, with a small bathroom off the kitchen. Three large bedrooms, a bathroom, and laundry room occupied the upstairs.

Not long after moving in, we realized the utility bills were very high. We investigated and discovered the outside walls had no insulation. The walls were old lattice-style slats covered with plaster. So we soon discovered that not only were we the new pastor and his wife—but we were also a construction crew. For the two years we lived there, we tore down the walls and took the slats off, insulated them, and put up sheet rock, mud, and wallpaper. Every time the heater came on during those days of renovation, the plaster dust blew all over the house.

The church building, a converted horse barn, didn't look much like a church. Windows and a large door had been previously added. The siding was still the corrugated tin from the barn, but carpet had been laid over the concrete floor. Rows of wooden benches, a pulpit, and a cross made it a small country chapel inside. In spite of these small beginnings, we couldn't wait to move in and fill up the church with people who wanted to get saved. Who cared if the church still looked like a barn? We could fix that later.

And God did fill it up with people who wanted to get saved!

An amazing first church experience put our faith to the test. God came through and honored our faith and the prayers of those who had kept the church open. Steve set out knocking on doors in the small rural town and inviting people to church. At first we had mostly children with special needs and neighborhood children who would be picked up in our van for Sunday school. Their parents were happy to have them occupied for a few hours away from home. One day I finally said to Steve, "If we're going to see the church grow, we're going to have to find some regular adult people too!"

Our first break came when two of the daughters of our main members asked me to take them out to knock on doors and invite people to church. At one house we found a young married couple named Ron and Nancy. They began attending church and went forward to pray one Sunday, asking Jesus to come into their hearts.

Ron came from a rough background. He had grown up around drugs and alcohol with little parental supervision. Theft and other minor crimes had become a way of life. He had met Nancy, a farm girl from a good home. After they were married, they moved to Monmouth for a new start. When Ron became a Christian, he decided he should make restitution for the things he had stolen. He contacted the Salvation Army about a safe he and a few of his friends had stolen. After emptying the contents, they had thrown it into the Mississippi River to get rid of the evidence. Teenage boys with a large safe would be easy to spot. Unfortunately, after reading Ron's letter asking for forgiveness, they contacted the police, and the police contacted Ron and directed him to turn himself in. Steve and Ron went to the town police department together.

Unfortunately, in our ignorance we did not realize that because he was arrested on a Friday, he would have to spend the weekend in jail. This is another example of how God turns a trial into a blessing. They took Ron to jail, but the local jail was full, so they moved him to another nearby jail. In this jail his brother was also detained for petty theft and drug use. Ron was so happy to see his brother and testify to him about what God was doing in his life. His brother got angry and slapped him around for it, but the gospel was presented to him.

Despite these hardships and wondering why this would happen, God would get the final word. A beautiful scene remembered by those in the courtroom is the day Ron stood before the judge, who asked him why he had written the letter asking for forgiveness and turned himself in. Ron's face lit up with a huge smile as he said, "Because I want to go to heaven."

Ron was given probation, had to pay for the safe, and was released.

The church began growing. Ron and Nancy were inviting their friends and relatives. On another Saturday, while knocking on doors, Steve met Frank and Anna and invited them to church. They didn't come right away, but one Sunday morning they filed in with their four children and Frank's two alcoholic brothers. We never thought to ask them about their legal status. It wasn't too long before they gave their hearts to God and were regular in their attendance. They were living in a house with Frank's brothers. Their whole family slept in one bedroom. They shared the living room and kitchen with Frank's two brothers.

Frank and Anna were both hard workers. After a few months they saved enough money to buy an old two-story house. To us it looked like a train wreck, to them a palace. Some of our fine church ladies learned a lesson in humility when we went over to scrape the grime off kitchen floors on our hands and knees and helped Anna clean the rest of the house before they moved in.

Word spread in the little town that something was happening in our little horse barn church. A local fisherman who ran a fish market started attending. Ron's cousins and others showed up. Steve baptized at least ten new Christians at camp. We were encouraged that new people were showing up and God was moving in our little town.

Trying to make ends meet, I promised God I would cook and eat whatever He provided. Most families had gardens and were anxious for us to have one too. One of the men from church came over and plowed up what looked like a football field to me for our garden. Having never raised a vegetable in my life, I didn't know where to start. Always good at making plans, we bought seeds and tomato plants and drew up a garden plan. I tried to plant things as the directions told me to. Then I realized I didn't have any tools. Someone gave us a hand plow called a row hoe. It was supposed to keep the ground turned up as you rolled it down the rows. We didn't have to water, because in Illinois it seemed to rain at just the right times. Everything started coming up, but I couldn't always tell a weed from a plant.

We did grow a few vegetables. Steve even planted cantaloupe, not knowing cantaloupes don't grow well in Illinois. One day when checking his cantaloupe plant, he was so excited when he saw an actual very tiny home-grown cantaloupe. He didn't stay excited for long because the next time he checked it, an army of little black bugs had found it. There would be no cantaloupe. We had a garden with corn, tomatoes, and a few potatoes. The main plants growing there, however, were very large uncontrolled weeds.

We probably ate healthier in Monmouth than at any other place before or after. The fisherman brought us the fish he didn't sell each day. Women in the church had pity on me and brought me their extra vegetables. I had to learn to can vegetables because we didn't have a freezer. One day Frank and Anna and their family were excited to butcher a cow. This meant every part of the cow was used. They didn't know I had promised to cook and eat anything God sent to us. They thought they were being generous when they brought me a big, ugly cow heart. Since it was a muscle, I reasoned in my mind that it would be tough. I remembered that when my mother cooked tough meat, she would cook it in tomato sauce. I put the heart in a pan, half-covered it with tomato sauce, and thought it would work. I found it hard to look at because it just looked to me like a big, bloody heart. After I boiled it to death, the only way I could get it down was to put it between two slices of bread and tell myself with each bite, "Roast beef . . . roast beef . . . roast beef."

I learned to be more careful with my promises.

One day Dennis, the boy we met in Davenport, showed up at our doorstep, having run away from home. With his mother's health failing and his father in jail, he needed a place to live. I think there might have been talk of placing him in foster care. He decided that *we* should be his foster care.

The child protection workers were contacted, and we filled out the forms to make it legal. By this time another son, Mark, had been born. We weren't really trained or prepared to raise a teenager. Our boys were five, four, two, and the new baby. We loved Dennis and wanted to see him have a happy Christian life. It was a crazy, fun-filled time. Dennis livened the place up for sure. One day I came home to find "Bob Nuthin"—a fake man—sitting on the couch with his legs crossed. Dennis had stuffed a shirt and a pair of pants with rags and other pieces of material and taken a bag to make a head. "Bob" had a hand-drawn face and wore a hat. Dennis had kept the boys entertained, holding pretend church services in the front room while I ran an errand.

Dennis didn't like school and started skipping classes. Circling down into old habits, he became unhappy and finally ran away from our house too. The one thing I had told him when he came was "If you run away from us, we won't let you come back." Dennis ended up in a number of foster care homes and lived at Boys Town at one time. Years later he contacted us, telling us that he had become a Christian. He had gone back to school and finished his education. Today Dennis has a wife and two children. We are still in contact with him. God takes our small efforts and is always faithful!

During our second year at Monmouth our church attendance ran between seventy-five and a hundred people on Sundays. We decided the time had come for the second big project, the horse barn church. Noticing a large brick school being torn down, we had a great idea. The Monmouth City Council had voted to tear down the beautiful historic building. Why not ask if we could have bricks and cover at least part of the church barn in brick? The demolition crew thought we were crazy, but they were happy for us to take all the bricks we wanted.

Every weekday after the men got off work, we met at the school site, took bricks off the building, and loaded them into trucks and trailers. Most of the bricks came off the sides of the building easily since the plaster was crumbling in between them. The bricks were beautiful, and our work drew us closer together with the common goal of making our building as appealing as possible.

Once we had the bricks we needed, they still had to be scraped and stacked before we could find a bricklayer. A time of excitement, spiritual growth, and friendship came from our time together scaping the bricks. We would sit around the yard by the church building cleaning the bricks as the dust from the plaster would cover us and make us look like coal miners.

Someone told us about an evangelist who also knew how to lay bricks. It was said, "E. E. Michael can lay bricks all day and preach all night." We contacted him to ask him to come and preach at a series of revival meetings. We also told him about the brick project. He accepted the call and would lay the bricks. Bricks would be laid during the day and the services would be held every night. Steve worked as the bricklayer's mud guy.

Brother Michael would lay a few bricks and yell, "Mud!" Then he would lay a few more bricks and again yell, "Mud!"

This went on all day. Even though Steve was only twenty-six, he had a hard time keeping up with this old guy.

The first weekend we had let the word out about the revival services and invited the students from the Bible college to attend. It would take them about an hour to drive down from the Quad Cities. We were expecting a big crowd that night. That day they ran late with the bricklaying. An hour before service time, Brother Michael left Steve to clean up. After cleaning up the brick-and-mud area, Steve realized there would be no time for a shower. He rushed to the house, wiped off the day's work as quickly as possible with a washrag, and put on his white shirt, suit, and tie. The large crowd was waiting for Steve to come open the service.

Sitting in the front row with the boys, I started worrying. Finally, one minute before start time, Steve walked into the church and went to the pulpit. He turned to face the crowd and there were a few giggles. I had to hold my face very straight or I would have laughed out loud.

As he faced the crowd and opened the service in prayer, he did not realize that he looked like a raccoon in a suit. Large blackish circles of brick dust around his eyes had been missed in his rushed cleanup. His clean white shirt also had black water spots around the neck. He turned the service over to the song leader and sat down next to me. I whispered and giggled that he should go back home and try again.

We lived in Monmouth for two years. The first year we baptized ten new converts at the summer camp meeting. The second year was filled with church growth and new people coming to faith. But the Midwest was like another world from the West Coast life, which we were much more familiar with.

On top of being homesick for Santa Cruz, we didn't know what to do with all the baby Christians. We knew how to guide people to find Jesus, but we didn't know how to take them deeper.

In a decision that we later regretted, we answered the call from the Santa Cruz church to be the assistant pastor and help with the mission. We were going home!

Chevette Scooter 1983

The Shepherd's Fold dinner

Elm St. Mission drawing

Sunrise Service

The Shepherd's Fold

Elm St. Mission, 117 Elm St.

Pen and Ink of Shepherd's Fold by Steve Washburn

Steve preaching at devotions at the Shepherd's Fold

The Palm family: Susan, Steve, and Larry

Sandy singing at devotions at the Fold

Elm St. veterans

Steve in 1967

8

THE SECOND TIME
IN SANTA CRUZ

We had high expectations about being the returning heroes in our move back to Santa Cruz. Going back turned out to be like grown children trying to go home to live with their parents. It was a disaster. We looked at ourselves as experienced adults with four children. Steve had been the pastor of a church, he had finished Bible college, and we were twenty-seven and twenty-six. Unfortunately, Wally and Beverly looked at us like inexperienced kids still needing a lot of help.

Wally found a house in Scotts Valley that had been red-tagged by the city. It looked like an unfinished home building project. The house had obviously been built by the previous owner. I don't think he cared much about things like building permits and inspections. It did have enough bedrooms for our four growing boys.

The original owner must have loved trees. The master bedroom had a tree growing in it. It had originally grown up through the roof, but by the time we moved in, there was a stump in the corner where the tree had been cut to build a second story. Our children, ages six, five, three, and two, thought it was great fun to run up and down the stairs and look at a tree in a bedroom. We drew the line when it came to watering it. While we lived there it received no water.

One day, to the delight of our boys, Wally brought us an old dog named Joe. Susan, Steve's sister, had moved back to Santa Cruz after becoming a Christian. Her husband's boat had been found drifting at sea with no one on board. Joe the dog was the only living survivor. She didn't have a place for a dog, so we were elected to have Joe come and live with us.

Joe was a comfort to our boys. He was old and arthritic but kind and loving. One of our boys, Andrew, told a friend that Joe was the best watchdog ever. "He just watches and watches!"

One day Joe disappeared. We never found out what happened to him. But he *was* the best watchdog ever!

While were in Iowa and Illinois, the ministry in Santa Cruz had grown. The Shepherd's Fold housed about twenty young people and there were also families now living in small cabins on the property. The pastor, Jerry Beck, and his family lived in one of the larger cabins, and Wally and Beverly had a separate living area attached to the main building.

In our absence and unknown to us, another man, Dan Free, had also been hired to help with the church and the mission to the street people. The church called Steve to be the assistant pastor and help with the mission work but had neglected to mention to us that Dan and his family had also been hired. The confusion came because two men were now in charge of running the mission. Anything with two heads has a problem. We realized the role of assistant pastor had a vague job description. An assistant pastor is whatever the pastor decides he will be. Pastor Beck and Wally decided Steve's schedule and he was asked to keep a time sheet to show what he did with each day.

Not long after we moved back to Santa Cruz, the church took possession of the whole building on Elm Street. The union offices moved out, so we now had access to the upstairs room, a back fellowship room, and a small kitchen. The kitchen did have a few weeds and grass growing up through the floor that we periodically cut and killed. The mission services could now be held in addition to the regular church services in their own area. Seven days a week we held a short preaching service in the back room and then distributed meals to anyone who came to the service. Sandwiches were given out at the gate for those who came late or who didn't want to attend the preaching and the singing.

Food was a problem, feeding not only the young people living at the Sheperd's Fold but also the growing mission crowd. By the end of each month the mission services had eighty to a hundred men and women attending seven days a week. At the beginning of the month the crowds weren't as large because many of the street people received disability checks. They would rent a cheap motel room, have parties, and then when the money ran out, they would show back up at the mission.

Wally belonged to the Rotary Club and knew people in the community. Through his local contacts, food for the mission came from some of the local grocery stores. He went to the stores where he knew the managers or someone who worked there and asked them if they had any food that they would like hauled off. Food products have expiration dates and cannot be sold after that date, so the stores were happy to have someone else take it away. Wally was experimenting with growing pigs and a milk cow, so at first they thought the food was going to the pigs. A small pickup truck was purchased and a rotation of two "Fold" residents took turns going to the stores every day. This job was forever after called the "pig run," even when there were no longer actual pigs.

The Fold was full of hungry mouths. Beverly, always thrifty, served oatmeal every morning. One morning in prayer she complained to God. "Lord, I'm really tired of oatmeal. Is there any way you could send us some eggs?"

Beverly told everyone she had prayed for eggs. Not much later someone came across a Mormon egg farm. The manager discovered that the eggs in one of their refrigerators had been overlooked and he thought they might be too old to sell. The owner asked the Fold if they would like to have some eggs. All we had to do was drive a truck to pick them up. Steve went to pick up the eggs in Watsonville. He thought he would load a few boxes of eggs and be done.

God certainly answered prayer. We had eggs, all right —11,000 of them! No one can ever tell me that God doesn't have a sense of humor.

We ate eggs in every possible way they could be cooked. We oiled the shells to make them last longer, served eggs whenever possible, and froze what we couldn't eat fast enough. Eggs were cooked and prepared with every recipe that we could think of that required eggs. We fixed scrambled eggs, fried eggs, boiled eggs, poached eggs, and had egg soufflé, quiche, puddings, pies, and casseroles. We ate everything *egg* for months!

Another animal encounter came with a nanny goat that I found wandering on a busy side road. The four boys and I were driving home one night from an evening service and saw a confused and upset goat running off and on to the road. I immediately pulled over to try saving it from being hit. The goat was very friendly and let me grab her collar.

Not knowing what else to do, I decided to put it into the back seat of the car. It was a blur of bottoms and legs as the three boys who had been sitting in the back seat dove to the front seat. After a little pulling, tugging, and sweet talk, I did get the somewhat reluctant goat into the back seat of the car. *What will I do with a goat?* I wondered.

We did have a backyard, so when we got home we tied her up there. The next day we took her to the Shepherd's Fold and put an ad in the paper and flyers around town to see if anyone would claim her. No one claimed the old nanny goat, so she turned into goat stew. Poor Nanny—she literally went into the ministry!

There was also a time when the Shepherd's Fold was running low on funds and Wally decided to try horse meat. After all, he reasoned, horse meat was eaten for food in Europe during the world wars, and by Native Americans. It must be edible. This cheap source of meat would feed the increasing number of people at the Fold. With only Wally's personal paycheck paying most of the bills, drastic measures seemed reasonable.

At the beginning of the first meat changes, Wally and Beverly took us to the shed, where an animal carcass hung, to tell us about the horse meat experiment. "We have something we want to tell you," Beverly said solemnly.

"*Horse!*" I cried out after they told us.

I had never heard of anyone eating a horse. The jokes at the dinner table were especially funny when new people who weren't told what they were eating ate with us. One of the new girls, Janelle, became an instant vegetarian when she found out. Growing up, she had ridden in barrel races at rodeos and loved horses. After eating a tasty roast, she nearly lost her dinner when she found out what she had just eaten for dinner.

Living communally sounds idyllic in the New Testament, but I wouldn't recommend it. Arguments and hurt feelings abounded. Young people suddenly felt led to pray when there was work to do. The meal preparation, outside work, maintenance, cleaning, canning, and sewing were often the times that tested even the most patient. In a time of revival people do whatever is needed to help people. This means working through the many emotional, physical, and spiritual problems involved in helping people who have thrown away the morals and norms of traditional American society.

Gradually things were changing. Wally and Beverly became more authoritarian. Even though the young people who lived at the Shepherd's Fold were adults, they were treated like the children they acted like. Steve and I were starting to ask how we would ever be looked at as adults.

We stayed for two years. Things had also changed for us. Although we loved the church and God's work in Santa Cruz, we wanted to be treated like adults. We realized that to Wally and Beverly we would always be kids who needed more help. It was time to pastor a church again and move away from home . . . again.

Some people have criticized Wally and Beverly for their methods. We now realize that even though some of their decisions were somewhat controlling and extreme, perhaps extreme circumstances called for extreme measures. I remind myself that there was no one else looking for two very mixed-up teenagers who needed Jesus. No one else lined up to help the hippies in Santa Cruz, feed them, tell them about God's forgiveness, and take them home.

Our mistake was that we had placed Wally and Beverly on a pedestal almost next to God and now realized that they were humans with faults and failings. I will be forever thankful that God sent Wally and Beverly into our lives to share their home, teach us to pray, and give us a solid foundation built on God's Word.

9

PHOENIX AND POMONA

We left Santa Cruz. Steve was asked to be the pastor of a small church in Phoenix. The house the church provided for the pastor and his family to live in had 800 square feet, two bedrooms, one bathroom, with a small kitchen and living room. It was a challenge to our growing family. We put two sets of bunkbeds in one bedroom for all four boys. The two redeeming features of the house were the large backyard that was fenced and had high oleander hedges on the back and sides for privacy, and a great air conditioner. Summer temperatures sometimes reach 110–115 degrees in Phoenix. The threat to encourage good behavior when the boys were fighting inside the small air-conditioned house was "If you boys can't get along, you'll have to go outside."

The was a small area for a table for two. Since there were six of us, we would need more room. The previous pastor had left a chest that would convert into a table. The front doors of the chest opened, and a table with legs pulled out to make it long enough. Table leaves were added that made it big enough for all of us to fit around the table. Folding chairs came with the set. When we put up the table, it stretched from the eating nook out into the living room. At each meal we opened the chest table to eat and afterwards took it all apart and made it a chest again. It is an understatement to say we lived in a very small space.

Living in the desert was a new experience. Irrigation water was turned on by the city to water the lawns. It gushed up from a large cement type of pipe and flooded the grass. The boys thought it was a great feature and we all played and splashed in the hot weather in what was probably not very clean water.

Phoenix was a time of trying to find our way without the cushion of the Shepherd's Fold. Two young women, Jan and Teena, were saved there. We held street meetings in downtown Phoenix and helped in a downtown mission that fed people. We tried encouraging the church that was already there and even convinced them to put an air conditioner in the church building. "We've been just fine with the swamp cooler," some said. We looked at air conditioning like a necessity, while some of the congregation looked at it like an extravagance.

One of the biggest challenges in ministry to small churches is finding a pastor who can support himself or herself while building the church. We were always counting our pennies and trying to make things work with what money we had. Steve received an invitation to be the speaker for a revival meeting. Meetings were held every night for a week to encourage people to reflect and be challenged to grow in their spiritual lives. The idea was also to evangelize the local community and bring new people into the church.

At the time we were pastoring in Phoenix, the boys were eight, seven, five, and two. The church that called Steve for the revival was in Wichita Falls, Texas. We went up highway 17 from Phoenix to Flagstaff to get on I-40 to take us to northern Texas. Having never seen Flagstaff, when we drove into that area area and saw the majestic San Francisco Peaks, we wondered why anyone would live in the Arizona desert when beautiful Flagstaff was also in Arizona.

The trip to Wichita Falls was a fourteen-hour drive in our Pinto station wagon. Steve had purchased a set of used radial tires to get ready for the long trip. Radial tires were supposed to be the best, so Steve was excited to find some that fit. What he didn't know was that radials needed to be mounted in a certain order, and the man who had mounted these tires had apparently done them backwards. We thought that we were good to go.

Somewhere in Texas on the second day, we had a flat tire. In the process of our changing the tire, the tire jack broke so we needed a new one. This put us behind schedule. We were up against the clock to be at the church by seven o'clock that night. We stopped at the first little town to look for a jack. Steve did not figure on the helpful but slow-moving Texan in the automotive store.

"W-e-l-l. . . we have several kinds of jacks . . ." he drawled slowly.

After a few minutes of dialogue even Steve was impatient and abruptly said, "Just give me that one!"

Back in the car, so far so good. We were going to be cutting it close, but we would make it to the parsonage to change and be ready for the first evening service. Suddenly the car started thumping—bump, bump, bump, bump. Another tire. Of course, I was yelling instructions for Steve to pull over. He decided the thumping must be from radial tire tread falling off, so he sped up to get the piece disconnected. After my not-so-patient comments, the kids shrieking, and a lot of thumping and shaking, it finally worked. Quiet again except for me.

Steve pulled over to check the damage. The tire seemed to be holding air, we had already used the spare, so we decided to move ahead. Besides, we had already spent our money on the jack, and there wasn't anything left to buy a tire. Plus, we were strangers in a strange land and wouldn't have known where to buy one if we had money.

More endless hours in a flat and dry countryside. Thump, thump, thump, thump, thump, thump. Another tire is going. Oh, no! It got the same treatment from Steve. Speed up, sling the rubber off the tire, and drive on. By now we were really running late. There wouldn't be time to make it to the parsonage, change, and get to the service by seven.

I instructed the boys to pass up one of the suitcases. As we were driving along, I helped the boys to change into their church clothes in the back seat of the car. Then I found my clothes, told the boys to close their eyes, and I changed in the front seat. Remember that all of this was happening as we were driving along with Steve and me in the front and four boys plus luggage in the back. Steve pulled over and we ran as if we were doing a fire drill, changed places, and I drove while he changed into his suit. Even with all our time-saving efforts, we were still going to be late.

At ten minutes after seven we arrived at the church. We could hear the singing, so we knew they had already started the service. In we filed. Of course, everyone watched us as they continued singing. There weren't any vacant seats in the back, so we had to walk single-file past the wondering eyes to the second row. Exhausted, I herded the boys to the pew in the front row. I felt hot and sweaty, tired but relieved. Steve walked to the platform and sat down to face the congregation.

The song service ended, and it was time for the special music. A man stepped to the pulpit to begin his song. I believe he thought he could sing opera style. In a country Texas church, this seemed a little out of place. As he sang, he made some awful faces for effect and his voice quivered on and on. I even remember the song: "The love of Go-ooo-od is greater, dee-eeee-per . . ."

By that time I was attacked with a fit of giggles. Everything gets funny when you're exhausted. I was now hearing little trickles from the boys. Whispering for them to be quiet while choking down my own laughter as the congregation looked on, I wondered if we should run for the door or try to contain ourselves. I didn't dare look at Steve sitting up on the platform.

I don't remember how we made it through, but Steve managed his sermon and we apologized for the delay and explained our troubles to an understanding congregation. On the way out of the church, the man who had sung stood shaking hands with everyone. When it was our turn to shake his hand, our five-year-old son, Ben, looked up innocently and said, "You make funny faces when you sing."

The kind and understanding man said, "Do I? I'll have to look in a mirror the next time I sing."

After church when we went to get in the car, we got a good look at the tires. Seeing the four flat tires with the metal showing, we thanked God that we had even made it at all. Looking back, we feel that God had to occasionally work overtime to keep us all alive. Despite all our old cars with used tires, we were never in a wreck. Amazing grace!

After a few years in Phoenix, a church in Pomona, California, called Steve to be their pastor. The church had a Christan school for the boys and a large two-story farmhouse for the pastor and his family. The property was spacious but not in the best part of town. From the upstairs windows of their bedrooms the boys watched the drug dealer who lived across the street and his visitors. One night there was even a stabbing and later the police showed up, lights blazing. The arrests and police work happened in real life. Who needed TV?

At Pomona while Steve pastored, I was hired to be a teacher at the Christian school. The principal, Ruth Swift, had quit her public-school principal job and started the Pomona Christian Day School. I knew I had a call to teach but had not completed my teacher training. Working with teenagers was a revelation. I remember one frustrated teen threw her sewing project onto the roof in frustration because it wasn't turning out right. At least our boys had a place to attend school where I knew what they were doing—most of the time.

In every ministry there are people who stand out. God takes the small things that we might do to give people an opportunity to have a life-changing experience with God. People don't always answer the call, but they know for sure that they had at least one chance.

A group of teenagers who went to the Pomona church wanted to do something for the Lord. We wanted to encourage their zeal, so it was decided to go to the houses in a few blocks' radius of the church and meet our neighbors. We set the date for a Saturday, gathered those who wanted to give it a try, and divided up the streets around our little church. Breaking into groups, we tried putting an adult with two or three younger people. The words that we encouraged them to say went something like "Hi. We're from the church right around the corner and we're out inviting our neighbors to visit our services and looking for children who might like to come to Sunday School."

We decided to go out for at least an hour and train our younger people about how it was done. I can usually talk to anyone, but some of the others were scared and a bit unsure of themselves. Although I was a little nervous myself, I didn't dare back down in front of kids who wanted to invite people to church. Not long after my group started knocking on doors, one of the girls from another group came running, yelling to me, saying, "Mrs. Palm—you have to come right now!"

Quickly walking to the next street over, I neared the little group and saw a large woman, at least six feet tall, towering over a couple of our teens. Our group looked very prim and proper next to this tall, boisterous woman. The look on their faces was something between shock and awe. To them she probably looked like a giant. Linda had on a pair of shorts, a sleeveless blouse, her hair in curlers, and she was talking in a loud voice swinging her arms in conversation. Laughing and telling the girls her life story, she made quite a sight. We learned that she had been raised in church but wasn't attending now. Our first impression of her was that she was an over-the-top, rowdy lady. Her first impressions of us were that she had never seen people with so many clothes on in the summer.

I came to the rescue and discovered that she and her husband lived right around the corner from our church. They had five children at home. She was so friendly and so real that I immediately liked her. A straight-shooter and a woman with a big heart, she was my kind of person. She was a long way from her church upbringing, and the Lord wanted something more for her family. I invited her and her family to church and told her a little about what it was like. Everyone was excited that day that we might get new visitors. I felt embarrassed that I hadn't really been excited about going door to door at first. It was such a great experience for our young people and a lesson for me.

The next Sunday Linda didn't show up, but a few Sundays later, in she marched: Linda; her husband, Gene; and their five kids! It wasn't long before the whole family was attending. She was the first one at the altar, and four out of five of her children went forward as well. Before long her husband went forward, and eventually they had all given their hearts to God. Their oldest son was already a teenager, and although he was a very nice-looking young man and extremely intelligent, he was in the stage where he wanted his own way.

For a while Linda and Gene's oldest son went to church with them. Later he got married and Steve performed the ceremony. This young couple were two teens who were on the wrong track. We tried desperately to hang on to them. The other children kept coming to church with Linda and Gene and became an important part of our lives. Sorrow seemed to follow Linda throughout her life, but she was always the one to help people in need, take in a wayward teen, or in my case, help a young mother.

Lest you think it was a totally happily-ever-after story, her oldest son ended up getting into drugs and killed a man in a rage. He has spent most of his life in prison. Her husband died of a heart attack, and their second daughter died in a car accident with a group of girls who had all been at a summer church camp. Linda kept going through things that would have broken other people. She herself had many physical challenges later in life but always took time to help people in need. One of God's special people, she will remain in my heart forever. I have lost touch with her three remaining children, but I know for sure that the efforts of a scared group of teens made a difference in her life. She gave each one of her family an example of someone who truly loved Jesus with all her heart, soul, mind, and strength.

During our time in Phoenix and Pomona, we bought and sold cars on a regular basis. It seemed that we were always buying and repairing an old car of some kind. We drove mostly old beater station wagons because they were big enough for our family. The current station wagon was in the shop at the Chevrolet dealership, and Steve met a car salesman named Phil. "What you need is a new car," Phil said.

Our current car was a 1977 station wagon Chevy Caprice. It was a great size for the six of us, but it guzzled gas and got about seven miles to the gallon. Steve and I discussed the prospect of a new car and thought we might be able to make payments instead of repair bills. We ended up going back to the Chevrolet dealership and asked for Phil. An enthusiastic car salesman, Phil was excited to see the whole family. He was originally from Australia, so he still had his amazing accent, plus oodles of enthusiasm to sell us a car. After giving Phil our information, he immediately had the car for us. (We were poor so you can imagine.) It was a brand-new Chevrolet Chevette Scooter, a stripped-down two-door model. For only $3,900, this new car would have no repair bills and get great gas mileage. Phil even offered to make the down payment! We signed on the dotted line to drive the car home and make payments for the next four years. A new car! Amazing!

At that time Matt was ten, Andrew eight, Ben seven, and Mark five. We never gave it a thought that it would be tough for all of us to travel in it and that the boys would not stay the same size. When we all got into the car, it seemed that it would work just fine for us: Steve and I in front, Matt, Andrew, and Ben in the back seat, and Mark in what we called "the wayback." The Scooter came with no trunk, but it had a hatchback set up with a back window. Mark at five looked at the "wayback" like his personal play area.

When one of the main church ladies saw us drive up in our new car, she made the remark, "Pastor Palm loves his family so much! If he goes to heaven while driving, he'll take them all with him!"

The denomination we were a part of had a district made up of churches in California, Arizona, and Nevada. Every year they met to elect officers and had a church campground not far from Pomona. A few months before the district meeting, Steve came home one day and told me that God had told him that he would be elected as the next district leader. I said something like "Oh, sure you'll be!" in full doubt mode.

That year they elected Steve to be the leader of the district. The district leader lived on the campgrounds during the year and was responsible for church problems, keeping and calling pastors for the churches, and leading the yearly camp meeting. Since though the denomination was not large, this would mean traveling to three states.

The Chevette would be perfect!

10

DISTRICT MINISTRY AND CHEVETTE STORIES

After being elected to the district, we moved from Pomona to the district campgrounds in Cucamonga, California. This meant moving from a large comfortable house to another train-wreck parsonage. Thankfully, the small house stood on five acres of land for the boys to explore. There were dormitories, a dining room, and a metal open-air building to hold the yearly services when the camp meeting was in session. One of the local churches met on the campgrounds on Sunday in a small chapel.

It seemed that the boys were always building a skateboard ramp, mowing lawns, digging a trail, or climbing a tree. When they weren't in school, they lived outside. Matthew, our oldest son, was musically gifted, so we had paid for him to take piano lessons when we lived in Pomona. The lessons were unsuccessful because he just memorized the songs that were assigned and didn't practice. During the time we lived at the campgrounds, however, he decided to teach himself to play the piano and spent hours in the dining hall, where there was an old piano. Today he is a senior pastor and an accomplished piano player.

We lived for a year on the campgrounds and felt God wanted us to move to Flagstaff, Arizona, to start a new church there. We rented a house and a small office building and started holding services. Another family moved to Flagstaff to help us start the church. As we worked together, new people were added to our little congregation and the church grew.

Jay and Rhonda were our first new contacts in Flagstaff. Rhonda's parents had sent us a letter with her address when they heard we were starting a new church in Flagstaff. Steve and I knocked on their door and found a rough group of people. Jay cut firewood for a living. He looked like a mountain man with a long, straggly beard and outdoor clothes and boots. Rhonda was such a quiet, soft-spoken person that she seemed lost and unsure of how to live in the world she had chosen. Steve and I introduced ourselves and invited them to the new church. We kept dropping in on them, and they finally came and gave their hearts to God. Later in their walk Jay became a pastor.

Our fifth son, Daniel, was born in Flagstaff not long after we arrived, in what is now called the "old Flagstaff hospital." At that time it was the only hospital in town. I noticed that he was a big baby with a big chest and looked a little blue. They took him away and ran tests. The doctor came back and told me he had an enlarged heart and they needed to fly him to the Phoenix Children's Hospital. The plane was small, so I would not get to go with him.

You can imagine how my emotions flew in all directions. There was no way I would stay in Flagstaff when my baby was in Phoenix. I signed myself out of the hospital, found someone to watch the other boys, and Steve drove us to Phoenix, which is about 140 miles from Flagstaff.

I began calling family and the Shepherd's Fold for help. Steve had to go back home and watch the boys and I wanted to stay in Phoenix with Danny. A church friend's mother had a home in Phoenix and made it available to stay in. The home stood empty in an old section of town not far from the hospital. It was furnished and ready because our friend's mother was away. A real problem occurred since, as much as I put on a superwoman front, I had just given birth and felt very weak.

Our Pomona friend Linda came to the rescue. She bought her own ticket to Phoenix on a Greyhound bus. These first days were a blur. The heart specialist ran a battery of tests on Danny, and I went every four hours through the day and night to hold Danny and feed him. I wanted him to know his mother would always be there for him and to give him a reason to get well.

In the natal ICU Dany looked like a giant baby. He weighed eight pounds, while most of the other babies were preemies or had more severe problems and were very small next to him. My legs were swollen, so Linda found me a wheelchair and faithfully pushed me all over the hospital down long corridors and up elevators to get to Danny every four hours. He had a temper from the beginning and a loud set of lungs. We could always hear him down the hall as we approached the ICU. He was hungry and let everyone know it!

One night after our hospital visit, in the process of unlocking the back door, I said to Linda, "Look! The kitchen floor looks so beautiful!" The moon shone through the window and the kitchen was lit up. The reflection of light made the floor shine. Opening the door, however, I stepped into several inches of water.

We had turned on the washing machine by the back door before we left for the hospital. It had backed up, overflowed, and flooded the kitchen with water seeping into the living room and soaking the carpet—just what I needed. We tried mopping it up, using towels and anything else we could find to clean up the mess. I would call Steve when he woke up and give him the bad news. How would we ever pay for the water damage?

God had gone before us even in this overwhelming crisis! The homeowner's insurance paid for the repairs—and even replaced the living room carpet. The owners later thanked us for our mishap and told us we could visit anytime!

Daniel had a heart valve that didn't close properly. The diagnosis was Epstein's anomaly of the tricuspid valve. His heart was enlarged because the oxygenated blood was mixed with the unoxygenated blood. The cardiologist told us Danny would need surgery in the future, but they hadn't come up with surgery that would fix it. It wasn't much comfort when the doctor said, "By the time your son needs the surgery, we will have invented the procedure." He told us just to let Danny do everything the other boys did and that his body would tell him when he had to stop. He didn't mention that his lips and fingernails would turn blue and that we would find him passed out in the snow. But the doctor didn't lie—when Danny needed the surgery in his twenties, it was available.

While in Flagstaff we learned the terrifying lesson that not all people can be helped. A family with four children began attending the church. We were used to ministering to strange people and believed that God could help anyone. This family had a very strange father and a mother. The little congregation tried to help them by renting a motel room for them for a few weeks. When that money ran out, they quit coming to church. We realized they were professional beggars and lived by going to different churches for financial help. Everyone they met was touched by their children and wanted to help, so we kept trying.

A few of the men from different churches kept in touch with them and tried to be faithful. One day one of the ladies in the church called and recounted a horrible story. The father of the family decided that one of his children had a demon, so he stuffed him into a suitcase and put him under the sink until he died. I'm not sure how he was found, but the police arrested the father and mother, and they are probably still in jail. The family who attended our church took the remaining children in as foster care children until they could be placed in more permanent homes.

The Flagstaff home mission church prospered, so a pastor to take our place was elected and we moved to Prescott, Arizona, to start another new church. While living in Flagstaff and Prescott, Steve still had to travel for the district to other churches and each summer to the campgrounds to hold the yearly camp meeting. During this time we had some exciting car stories. We call them the Chevette stories.

They are funny family stories when we retell them today—but they were no fun at the time!

The Chevette stories were a result of Steve's herculean efforts to travel to places with our family, get things done, and be able to pay for it. Three years after we purchased the first Chevette, we decided that we needed a four-door vehicle with a little more room. We had made the payments faithfully, so our credit was good for Chevette number two. The new car had four doors and air conditioning. We might be cramped, but at least we would be cool. Before the reader gets too irate about safety issues, please remember that seat belts were nonexistent or rarely used, and child car seats had not yet been invented.

In July our yearly summer church camp meeting was scheduled, and since Steve was the district leader, he oversaw the campgrounds and any work projects that needed to be done to be ready for camp. This year a remodel of the building where we held the church services was in progress. Water misters and fans were being installed to cool off the metal building and make the hot summer California day services more comfortable.

It was the summer of 1983. We were getting ready to drive to Cucamonga, California, before camp to work on the building. Steve came home from the local discount hardware store with ten ceiling fans and two lawn mowers that he had found at a "not to be passed up" price. I stared at the pile with unbelief and of course asked him how he was going to get all of us and the pile of fans the 350 miles to Cucamonga.

"We'll figure out something" was the answer that I had grown accustomed to.

I don't remember the exact words, but I was always quite well spoken when it came to telling him how crazy he was and how he would never get it done. Steve never said much but has always just quietly gone about doing what he thinks needs to be done. I didn't want to even think about it, so I just concentrated on getting the clothes washed and packed.

When the day to load the car and leave came, I couldn't believe my eyes. Steve had already added a trailer hitch to the car and purchased a used Coleman clam shell trailer. Structurally the trailer was sound, but it looked as if it had been through a few wars as far as the paint job. It was a sort of nondescript tan color. I can still see it in my mind, but it almost defied imagination. Picture this: the four-door Chevette with the clam shell trailer hitched to it. A top carrier on top of the Chevette roof loaded up. The clam shell was loaded, and the lid closed. On top of the clam shell trailer were more boxes tied down to it. Plus, put Steve behind the wheel, me in the front holding the baby, Danny. Matt now thirteen, Andrew eleven, Ben ten, and Mark seven. The gas tank was full, two weeks of clothing ready, ten ceiling fans, and a lawn mower. Ready to go!

Well—almost.

We left Prescott and were traveling down Highway 60 on a two-lane road near Quartzsite. Five miles from the interstate, one of the boys let out the yell "Dad!" Mark later told us that about six inches in front of his face in the wayback window, he had seen the top carrier sliding down the back of the car.

I looked in the rearview mirror in time to see it hit the trailer and bounce and spin down the middle of the road behind us.

We pulled over as quickly as possible. Fortunately, there was no other traffic near us. Matt, Andrew, and Steve ran back. To their amazement, the load was still strapped solidly in place, minus the carrier legs, of course.

On the side of the road they took everything off the clam shell top, strapped on the top carrier that had just taken the road trip, and repacked everything else on top of that. The load on the clam shell was now about three feet higher than the Chevette roof. Because of the wind drag, we could travel only about fifty miles an hour with the gas pedal floored. We received some strange looks from passing cars but fortunately we weren't pulled over. I'm glad that the highway patrol officers were doing other things that day.

We finally arrived at the campgrounds about six hours later. If the boys were embarrassed before to be seen with us, they now realized that it could always be worse. Steve had done it—the ceiling fans, lawn mowers, and family had arrived in one piece. But it would have made the Beverly Hillbillies blush.

During the time Steve served as the district leader, moving became a normal event and we were well acquainted with local U-Haul businesses. First we left Pomona to move to the district campground, then from the district campground to Flagstaff and then to Prescott to new start churches. Moving back to the campground became the default.

On one move Steve had gone by the campground house a few days before we were moving back from Flagstaff. He noticed a few bugs but didn't realize it was an infestation. I suggested that he set off some bug bombs before our arrival. Problem solved, right?

Steve drove the U-Haul truck and I drove the Chevette the 400 miles from Flagstaff to Cucamonga. We got a late start, so we didn't pull in until about 10:00 p.m. It was dark, and we had been driving all day after the last packing and cleaning. I was totally exhausted. Steve, tired himself, dealt with the boys, who were naturally cranky from being cooped up all day in the car. I opened the front door of the house and turned on a light. When I screamed, Steve and the boys came running. There all over the floor of the empty house was a sea of roaches and bugs on their backs. What looked like thousands of tiny feet in the air, with some of them still wiggling, was the final straw. Before we could even sleep, we had to clean up hundreds of roach carcasses and move some furniture in.

I wasn't about to sleep on that floor!

Once again while living at the campgrounds I had the brilliant idea that I needed a dog. There would be plenty of room for the dog to run, and the boys would like to have a pet to grow up with. My family always had a dog when I was growing up. My mother at one time raised boxers and had a few litters of puppies, so I decided I needed a boxer puppy. I did not realize when I thought about our family dogs how they had become so well trained—it was because my parents had put in the time it takes to have wonderful dogs.

I named the female puppy Katy. In an all-male household, I thought it would be nice to have another female for company.

Looking back, I really don't know what I was thinking! Raising a dog is like raising a child. It takes constant attention and is time consuming. When we decided to travel, it meant another body in the Chevette.

Of course, the time came for a trip. District leaders were required to attend meetings when they were needed for general church business. An emergency meeting came up that Steve would be required to attend in Rock Island, Illinois. We decided we would go to Grand Junction, Colorado, where my parents were now living, and drop the boys off so that we could attend the meeting. We realized that adding the dog to an already-crowded car would not work. By this time when someone said, "road trip," I nearly broke out in hives. I convinced Steve I needed to fly to my dad and mom's house, where I would meet him.

That meant he would have five boys and a dog in the car. Steve had to go to the meeting, my parents would provide free babysitting, so why not? Before they left home, Steve found another one of his "not to be passed up" deals on two-liter bottles of soda at a great discount. Thinking of how much the boys would enjoy the soda, he bought twenty-nine of them.

For the trip from Cucamonga, California, to Grand Junction, Colorado, clothes for a week, five boys, twenty-nine two-liters bottles, and a dog were piled in the Chevette. They stopped often for bathroom needs and to walk the dog, but it was still a miserable trip. The soda bottles were piled around the boys on the floor and in every possible opening. To make matters worse, the dog was having gas problems. Holding their noses and yelling for open windows was interspersed in between the usual brother fussing that takes place on a long trip.

To add to the misery, in Utah a highway patrolman pulled Steve over for speeding. "Registration and license, please," the officer recited after Steve rolled down the window.

The officer looked at the scene. Five boys, a dog, twenty-nine two-liter bottles of soda, and a very frazzled father looked back at him. "Where are you headed? Are you planning on getting there tonight?" he asked. He handed Steve back his registration and license, ending with "Drive a little slower."

When Steve retells the story he always says, "The Mormon Church and large families are common in Utah. The officer must have understood and had pity on us."

Steve served as the district leader for six years. His traveling took a toll on our family. We were without a father in the home for long periods, and as hard as I tried, it wasn't the same for the boys. Our second son, Andrew, was a very sensitive boy of thirteen. He often went through being compared to our very talented oldest son and had a hard time with all the moving and being without his father at home.

We prayed for Andrew and wisdom for our family.

God knew the future—and sent the answer.

11

MICHIGAN

A church in Michigan with a good reputation for being a strong church called Steve to be their pastor. We thought that this would be a chance to shore up the family and provide stability for the boys. Once again we packed up a U-Haul truck and in two vehicles moved to Michigan. For the second time we experienced the reality that life on the West Coast is a different world from life in the Midwest. Although we met some very kind and genuine people, there were also those in the church who were legalistic and frowned on what they considered our "worldly" ways. The church in Michigan was a family church—mainly one family. Of the seventy people who were the regulars, I think thirty-six of them were related. They were so conservative that some of the ladies didn't believe that we should wear sandals. I have always thought that feet were not the most beautiful part of the anatomy and wondered what they would have thought of Jesus and the disciples wearing sandals. The first impression of their new pastor and family was that they were "worldly."

"Worldly" ways consisted of things like wearing open-toed sandals and letting our boys wear baggy below-the-knee surfer pants. Word spread that the new pastor let his boys wear shorts. The day we drove up to the parsonage, Steve had on a cowboy hat, a down vest, and I had on Birkenstocks.

What have we here? they thought.

What have we done? we thought.

The state of Michigan offers wonderful outdoor activities. The boys were able to hunt, fish, swim, and ice skate. We loved the Michigan outdoors but were a little worried about the church. That didn't make any sense since the church was the reason we were in Michigan.

We lived in a very well-kept two-story parsonage next to the church. The church building itself looked like a traditional Midwestern Christian church minus the steeple. A large yard with grass, decorative bushes, and trees surrounded the perfectly maintained buildings. Of course, the pastor's family was expected to be the custodians and do the yard maintenance.

Our first major decision involved where the boys would go to school. The public schools in 1986 when compared to today's education issues would seem very conservative, but we already worried about the anti-Christian rhetoric and the peer pressure the boys would face in public schools.

We made the choice early on to send our boys to Christian schools. Through the years some of the schools were wonderful and some not so great. I even tried home schooling, which was a disaster. Four boys in different grades, Danny, a toddler running around the house, and constant ministry interruptions made it impossible.

A well-known Christian school in Cincinnati, God's Bible School, had a high school that offered a boarding school. Matthew, always a good student, was sent to go to school there. I cried buckets sending my sixteen-year-old off to school, but we were trying desperately to do the best for our children. We were poor and were able to pay the tuition and room and board because they gave a scholarship for pastors' families. Matt had to work and basically fend for himself for anything extra. It turned out to be a very hard lesson in growing up for him, but he flourished, made friends, and met his future wife at school.

We discovered a Christian grade school in a nearby town for Ben, Mark, and Danny to attend. The pastor and his wife from a small Baptist church operated the Baymont Christian School in a town close by. They used what was called an A.C.E. curriculum for their school, which stood for Accelerated Christian Education. Students were able to study at their own pace and earn rewards for getting their work done. Ben, greatly motivated by rewards of extra recess and personal down time, finished a year and a half of school work in one year. He became motivated in his education, and both he and Mark learned to overcome their shyness to sing and speak in front of people. Mark used to cry when asked to get in front of an audience. When Mrs. Pierpont found out Mark had a good singing voice, she assigned him to sing a solo in a school program. He later became a worship leader. Danny started kindergarten and was just happy to be a big boy going to school. Pastor and Mrs. Pierpont will never know what an impact their ministry had on Ben and Mark.

What to do to help Andrew became a major challenge. He became increasingly rebellious and withdrawn. The window in his bedroom led to the roof, and he discovered he could go out the window onto the roof and climb down the side of the house to go out and explore the night.

Because the Christian life to us was such a life-changing gift, we thought our children would automatically want to be Christians. Andrew had different ideas. It was especially difficult for me, because as he was growing up, Andrew was my sweetest and most helpful son. If I was not feeling well, Andrew would be the only one in the family who would figure out that I needed help. He jumped in and helped in whatever way I needed, often without being asked.

After Andrew was caught sneaking out one night, Steve came down hard on him, and Andrew ran away. Imagine our pain as parents. We tried finding help for Andrew but discovered that unless you had substantial financial means, the programs to help teens were for teens who had broken the law or been placed in the state system. I asked Andrew if we had done anything to hurt or disappoint him in our Christian lives.

"Mom, if I believe that anyone is a Christian, you and Dad are. I just want to have my own way."

Andrew was a negative influence on the boys, especially on Ben. He and Ben had been the closest brothers. It was a sad time for our family, and we were desperate for answers. We finally gave him money to rent a room for a month, and he was supposed to find some work and pay his way afterwards. In full party mode at fifteen, he wasn't prepared for life. He maintained his apartment for a few months and then hit the road with a traveling carnival. He kept in touch with me and would call to tell me all the terrible things he was doing. I would assure him of my love and always offer him a home if he wanted to change. The phone calls would end, and I would cry and pray.

Time went on and Andrew drifted from place to place. We never knew for sure where he lived or how he survived. One Sunday he surprised us and came to church. My first thought when I saw him was horror and embarrassment. It was his rock star look. His blond hair ratted to spread out in a balloon around his head, falling past his shoulders. He wore skintight leopard pants with chains hanging from different parts of his clothing. He completed his ensemble with eyeliner, mascara, and an earring. He brought a girlfriend with him who looked a little better. Of course, they sat toward the front with the family to hear his dad's sermon and be seen.

After the traditional Sunday dinner, I still hadn't recovered. I did get a chance to testify to the girlfriend and she admitted that we weren't as awful as Andrew had told her we were. When they got ready to leave, we prayed with them, and I went to my bedroom. I fell on my knees, and as only a desperate mother can pray, I prayed. I asked God to forgive me for being embarrassed. I had been thinking of myself instead of his lost condition. I cried and sobbed and told God about my pain and finally got around to Andrew's pain. In my mind's eye I was given a beautiful picture of Jesus coming into the room. He knelt beside me at my bedside, put His arm around me, and told me that Andrew would find God. That experience has been one of the anchors of my faith. I watched the way that God did what He said He would do.

We lived in Michigan two years. Matthew graduated from high school and went on to college. Andrew moved to Colorado to live with my parents. He didn't like their rules either but managed to get his GED and joined the Army Reserves. When he returned to Colorado from his army training, he enrolled in Mesa College, completed a semester there, and joined the Marines. The joke around our house was "Andrew didn't like our rules, so he joined the Marines!"

In the following years before Andrew's salvation, when I would see him I would always have inner peace and faith that God would answer my prayer. I had met with God that day and He had given peace and faith to my broken heart.

God makes all things beautiful in His time! That time for Andrew began in the Marines as they went to Mogadishu, Somalia, in support of Operation Restore Hope in 1992. As part of the quick reaction force supporting the 11th Marines, Andrew found himself at checkpoint K-4 providing security for one of the busiest intersections in the city. During the second day of a forty-eight-hour rotation, a convoy of Somali military soldiers, whom he later found out were General Aideed's personal bodyguard detachment, approached the checkpoint. Andrew jumped off his fifty-caliber mounted Humvee with only his M-16 rifle and stopped the entire convoy in the middle of the street. For a few tense moments that seemed like an eternity, a standoff took place between Andrew and around twenty heavily armed soldiers. In the process he realized that no one else could see him and that he was standing there alone. God used that experience to show him clearly how short his life could be. After he rotated back to the safety of the airport, Andrew began contemplating what it would be like to meet God. He began praying because he knew he was not ready for that meeting. It has been a winding road for Andrew—but he is a Christian today.

The Michigan congregation was a classic example of an ingrown church, made up of four generations from one family. Steve preached quite a few sermons on gossip and spent a lot of Sundays in the Psalms, probably for his own encouragement. We knew some of the church members were complaining about that and everything else. We laughed when it came to the surface in the once-a-month children's story in the Sunday morning service. The kindly man giving the illustration had a telephone to his ear pretending to be talking to someone complaining. "I know, I know," he said. "Pastor Palm has been in the Psalms for a lot of Sundays. But remember: Moses and the children of Israel were in the wilderness for forty years." About that time a little girl grabbed the phone wire and blurted out, "You aren't talking to anyone! The phone isn't even plugged in!"

Theoretically the members wanted new people to get saved. In reality they wanted to keep everything nice and tidy. Unsaved people are messy.

We were so excited when we signed up eighty children for a summer Vacation Bible School. On Sunday after Bible study time was completed, we reached an all-time high for church attendance. The unchurched parents came to see their children's program and pick up the crafts they had made in VBS. After the comments from some of the regulars complaining that the spirit in the church changed because there were so many sinners present, we knew then that we weren't going to make it. We wanted all the sinners who would come!

12

ANOTHER ROUND
IN SANTA CRUZ

Trouble for the denomination we served came in the form of increased legalism. With our California background, people always came first for us. The church back in Santa Cruz stressed evangelism, prayer, and holy living. They weren't going to settle for a truckload of rules that didn't always make sense. The most recent rule forbidding the use of the Internet was the final blow. Politics in the church became an issue, and who you knew became more important than who you were. The Santa Cruz people who started the church from nothing felt they wanted to leave the denomination and become independent. This would allow them to keep their vision and the mission of the church. The church voted to call Steve to be their pastor.

Once again we loaded up our possessions and headed for California, back to our people, back to what we knew and were comfortable with. Our family moved into the church parsonage and began working in the community. Ben, Mark, and Dan were still at home. The church did indeed vote to become independent and left the denomination.

When our current church organization in Santa Cruz, part of the Bible Missionary Church, left the denomination to become an independent church, those who left walked away from the buildings and parsonages that many of them had helped to build. The church had never been a traditional church, and the work of the Shepherd's Fold was intertwined with everything having to do with the Santa Cruz church. The independent church became known as the Elm Street Mission.

It is always surprising to me when seemingly every person who ever donated a dollar to a church thinks he or she should have a say. The main families who had started the Santa Cruz church before it had a building were still attending. They had sacrificed and given themselves and their finances to the work for almost twenty years now.

The Shepherd's Fold was in transition. Wally and Beverly now both had health problems. The Fold was filled to the brim, the Elm Street Mission serving the homeless was going strong, and they were physically tired. I think Wally believed that he could still be Steve's father figure and things would go the way he wanted them to go. Since Wally was a big financial supporter, he assumed he knew what was best for the church, not realizing that Steve had grown up.

This was the beginning of the damaged relationship that would cause huge pain for all of us. In our hearts Wally and Beverly were on a pedestal almost at the right hand of Jesus. They had reached out to us when we were lost, provided us a home, fed us, and given us a place to belong. Wally was an extrovert with funny songs and ditties that we all repeated. One example was a song he sang at bedtime:

"To bed, to bed," said Sleepyhead.
"Tarry a while," said Slow.
"Put on the pot," said Greedy Gut.
"We'll sup before we go!"

Even with Wally's often biting criticisms, we loved him and still wanted to please him. Beverly, the mother figure, prayed for us and loved us. She was the spiritual rock we all wanted to be.

Wally and Beverly approached us about taking over the Shepherd's Fold. They would move to another location and perhaps take in a few people. They wanted to slow down. Wally had retired from his lucrative job in Palo Alto and now sought a quieter life.

At some point in this process Wally realized that he would not have enough money to retire. They had never taken a salary during their years running the Shepherd's Fold, so they decided they deserved retirement and would sell the property and move, retaining financial control of the Shepherd's Fold Ministries. They asked another couple to take over their responsibilities at the Fold until the property could be sold, not talking to us about this decision. We believed that the church and the Fold were God's work and didn't belong to anyone individually. Wally stopped supporting the church, so Steve had to go to work.

It is a hard but necessary lesson to learn that your heroes are human.

The first job interview Steve had turned out to be a humbling experience. His theology degree and pastoral training were not helpful in getting a secular job in Santa Cruz, a very liberal town. In fact, those would be a hindrance. He finally was able to land a truck driving job at Odwalla Juice Company, which had been started by a few eccentric entrepreneurs who didn't care how religious Steve was as long as he could do the job. Later his brother, Larry, wanted some of his land cleared, so he asked Steve to chop down trees he marked. Steve cleared the land in exchange for the wood, so he was able to make a decent income selling cords of wood and got into great shape at the same time. The boys and several of the mission guys were hired to be his helpers. Being a lumberjack was hard work but a great pressure-reliever.

Wonderful things came from this time in our lives. The boys were growing up. Ben and Mark were teenagers and discovered surfing. They spent their time between school, surfing, and working for their Uncle Larry, who had become a well-respected mountain surveyor. They reconnected with their cousin David, who became a regular fixture at our house. David and Ben worked for their Uncle Larry on surveying projects in the Santa Cruz mountains, working and surfing together.

Ben, Mark, and Danny served at the mission handing out sandwiches, clothing, and blankets. They experienced the blessings of giving to those who were less fortunate. Making friends with some of the men who came regularly showed them what addictions to drugs and alcohol and bad decisions can do to a person's life. The time in Santa Cruz affected the boys for life. They grew up knowing that we are saved to serve.

An especially mischievous trick was played on me during that time. Ben and David were headed off to work early one morning and I got up to see them off. As they headed out to the car, I greeted them from the door to tell them to have a good day and to be careful. I should have known that something was off because they both had funny looks on their faces.

On the way back to the bedroom I almost stepped on the coiled rattlesnake lying in my bedroom doorway. I screamed and jumped right into the middle of the bed. Water beds were popular at that time, and we had one. Steve got to ride on the waves as I screamed and jumped on top of his sleeping form. What a way to start the day! The rattlesnake was dead, but it certainly fooled me. The boys were not so happy when Steve finished giving them a piece of his mind.

We encouraged the boys to be a part of the youth group at the Santa Cruz Bible Church, another church in the area. There were no other teenagers except their cousins in our church at the time. On one of their youth group mission trips to Mexico, Mark was called to be a missionary.

I went back to San Jose State to finish working on my teacher's credentials. I rode the bus down the winding Santa Cruz Highway to get to my classes since there were no online classes available at that time. As the older returning student, I always stuck out. I made friends with the younger students, who were always happy when I shared my lecture notes.

I have always loved school, so I worked hard and graduated with honors. Unlike today, my fellow students and professors showed respect for my conservative Christian beliefs. If I had a logical and well-thought-out reason to share, I never felt isolated from the academic discussion that I so loved.

At graduation I put my foot in my mouth as usual with a professor I admired. She was a seasoned professor who had spent her life studying amber, fossilized tree resin, in ancient artifacts. I never thought of her as being old and greatly admired her. As we stood in line for the opening processional by department, she stood there in her beautiful regalia with a medieval hat with a tassel that looked like lacy gold. I admired it and said, "Your tassel is so beautiful. It must be an antique."

She looked at me, chuckled, and replied, "Well, I guess it is." I had inadvertently just called my professor an antique!

One of the most heartbreaking parts of ministry to the homeless is seeing what a life of drinking and drug abuse does to people and their families. Since Vietnam was our war, we met and became close to a number of the Vietnam veterans living on the streets of Santa Cruz. This was a time before organizations like Tunnels to Towers. Many of the soldiers from Vietnam came home to ungrateful crowds who mocked and spit on them. Some came home addicted to drugs. Not much was known about post-traumatic stress disorder, and these veterans lived on the street banded together in their experiences and needs. They were always respectful and helped us when they were able.

During one mission service before the meal a very drunk mission guy got really loud and disruptive. Steve was preach-

I LIFT UP MY SOUL

ing and asked one of the vets named "Sarge" to help the guy out. Sarge got behind the guy, lifted him straight up out of the church bench, and threw him out the back door. Of course, when Steve had asked Sarge to help, he imagined a little easier and softer exit for the drunk man.

Bobby was another regular mission man who was a Vietnam veteran. He hung around the mission for a number of years and sometimes tried rehab centers and attempts to reunite with his family. We could only pray and leave these men in God's capable hands and hope that before they left this earth they were able to find God and make peace with their past. We loved them and tried to live God's love before them.

This time of ministry in Santa Cruz was very stressful. Steve was working his secular job and pastoring the church and the Elm Street Mission. Ben decided that he wasn't going to be a Christian and looked for a non-Christian girl, figuring that the place to find a girl like that was at the local skating rink, where he met a girl named Tiffiny, a senior in high school who lived not too far from the parsonage.

A rule at our house was that if you lived at home, you had to go to church on Sundays and be at Sunday dinner. Ben's answer was to bring Tiffiny to church and dinner. He decided that he wanted me to teach her to cook, so we started with learning how to bake a pie. Not too long after Tiffiny started attending and hanging out at the Palm house, she decided that she needed the Lord and became a Christian. How we laughed with God over this!

In one of our low points, a drunk mission guy who had to be removed from a service grabbed a piece of firewood and chucked it through the plate glass window at the back of the building. It barely missed one of the ladies sitting inside and brought the service to a halt. It was going to cost more money to fix the window than we had, so we boarded up the window until we could raise the money to fix it.

Two men came to the gate of the mission. They tried pretending that they were street guys but did a terrible job of convincing us. They finally confessed that they belonged to another church in town and were checking us out. Bill and Andre became great helpers and financial supporters of Elm Street Mission. With little financial support, we were unable to do the repairs that were needed on the building. Fewer people were coming to church, and the mission became the main outreach. Andre helped us and found the financial means to install a commercial-style kitchen in what had been two small office rooms. The men took down a wall to combine the two rooms and make them big enough to hold the new stove and counters. God is faithful when we depend on Him. When we are helpless, He isn't!

One day in 1989 while the boys were at work and Danny was asleep on the front room floor, the house began waving and shaking. My sewing machine bounced out of the cupboard onto the floor and some of the kitchen cupboard contents fell out as well. The parsonage, located in Soquel, was about a mile from the epicenter of the Loma Prieta earthquake. We went three or four days with no water or electricity, and there were long lines at the stores for batteries and water. It was amazing how nice everyone was to their neighbors in the time of this crisis. The drivers were courteous even though most traffic lights were simply blinking. In California that was a miracle!

The damage to the house from the earthquake was minor, but part of the Oakland Bay Bridge collapsed and many of the old buildings in Santa Cruz were destroyed. Our church building on Elm Street in downtown Santa Cruz stood firm. Constructed in 1912, it sustained only a few cracks, while the massage parlor across the street totally collapsed. Steve's brother, Larry, an engineer, checked the church out and showed that the foundation would have crumbled if the quake had lasted a few seconds more. The city sent people around to check the downtown buildings—and the church passed inspection.

After completing my bachelor of arts degree in history, I had returned to San Jose State to work on my teacher certification. After completing my course work and before being assigned to a high school for student teaching, I contracted meningitis. I had thought I simply had the flu. One morning Steve was getting ready to go to work and felt impressed by God that he should stay home. It was a good thing that he did. The doctor later told him that if he had gone to work that day I would have died. I lost consciousness, and Steve had a terrible time cleaning me up and getting me into a fresh nightgown. He laughingly told me later that I had one arm in and one arm out of my long flannel nightgown. He put me into the car as best as he could and drove me to the emergency section of the hospital. Unconscious people quickly get the attention of the emergency room nurses and doctors, so they wheeled me right in. About that same time the head of the communicable disease department for the county walked into the emergency room. He ordered them to do a spinal test, and the meningitis was quickly diagnosed. Because of God's care of me, I am not a vegetable or already in heaven.

After I recovered I completed my student teaching and received my California teacher's certification. We now decided that it was time to move again. Having stayed long enough in Santa Cruz to know that the mission work would continue, we felt that our work there was finished. It was time for a change, but the unknown was a little scary.

Before we left Santa Cruz, one of the men from the mission who was a regular paid us a compliment, telling us that he would miss us: "Steve is a man of the Word and teaches us—and in a way you can understand." It was the end of an era.

13

ARIZONA OR BUST

We decided to move back to Arizona, so I began looking for a teaching job there and we started saving money. We would have no help with moving expenses this time. For the first time since we began ministry, there would be no church to support us and no Santa Cruz position to return to.

Getting ready to move should have been easier. Matthew was now a married man. Andrew was in the Marines, Mark was working on his airplane mechanics license, and Ben had decided to run from God. Only Danny was still at home. He would be starting seventh grade in school. I landed a job at a new Christian school starting up in Cottonwood, Arizona. Cornerstone Christian Academy would be a middle and high school with grades seven through twelve. I was hired to teach history for all grades.

We decided to load only the essentials into Steve's truck, which had wooden sideboards where the cords of wood had been stacked. There would be no furniture until we rented a place to put it. We took beds, dishes, and clothes for this first exploration trip. Our furniture would follow later.

As usual Steve piled the truck as high as was humanly possible and tied it all down with multiple ropes and straps to hold it steady. We decided to drive the first day to Steve's aunt's house in Glendale, California, and then on to Arizona. In Arizona a temporary landing spot had been found. It was a studio one-room cabin that someone who was associated with the Christian school had built in the back area behind his house.

Setting off the first day of our trip to Arizona, I followed Steve in the old white Ford we used as a second car. Steve drove the loaded wood truck. The Ford had recently started overheating at times, and Steve's way to fix the problem was to load several plastic gallon milk jugs filled with water into the back seat. We had to stop every now and then to add water to the radiator. When we were close to Glendale, I realized that I did not know how to get to Steve's aunt's house. The traffic was getting congested, so I followed Steve as closely as possible.

It turned out that he wasn't sure which road to turn off on either. At the last minute he pulled quickly off the freeway. I tried following but had to drive across a marked-off area that separated the right turnoff lane from the rest of the lanes moving forward. Almost immediately I saw flashing lights and heard the siren from a police officer. By then the car was starting to overheat again.

When I rolled down the window to talk to the officer, I burst into tears. "I've been driving all day, I lost my husband, my car is overheating, and I don't know where I am!" I wailed. The kind officer took pity on me and helped me figure out how to get to where I was going. He didn't give me a ticket either! I pray the Lord blessed him for his kindness that day.

Steve's aunt got a kick out of seeing the big black lumber truck filled about ten feet in the air. We finally made it to the studio cabin in Cottonwood. Unloading the contents of the truck into the small building was interesting. We were on an adventure and wondered what God had in store for us. Not long after we arrived, the monsoon season hit Cottonwood. In July the usual weather is rain and magnificent lightning storms. We would put chairs in the back of the truck and watch the lightning for entertainment. We tried sleeping in the back of the truck bed, but the wind and rain would come up and send us running for the cabin.

Not long after school began, we were able to locate a house to rent. Finding a church was another matter. Having pastored churches for over twenty years now made it difficult for Steve to fit in, simply being a part of a congregation and not in a place of leadership. We did meet some wonderful Christians from several of the churches we visited and finally joined a church that was doctrinally like that of our first experience with the gospel.

A time of radical change had come to us. There were no rules about where to go or what to wear. We knew what we believed, and our faith in God did not waver, but we were praying that God would show us the difference between what came from God and what came from people. I realized that any outward thing itself like a gift of the Spirit or a certain way to dress was not what made us Christians. Only the love for God that gives us hearts of obedience can give us a right relationship with God. A complete surrender of our wills to live in God's way is what brings continuing peace and joy in serving God. Our relationship with God has to come from the inside, not the outside.

While we were on this learning curve with God, I taught school and Steve did various odd jobs. I eventually became the principal of Cornerstone and Steve became the pastor of the church we were attending. I decided to return to college for graduate studies.

One day Ben called from Colorado. He had kept in touch with my parents, who lived there, but mostly spent his time drinking and partying. He also called occasionally. This call was different. "Mom," he said, "I need to get saved. Can I come home?"

Of course, the answer was yes! We had prayed daily for Ben, but unknown to us, God had been at work. By the time he called me he was so under conviction that he was having dreams of falling into hell. Many times we pray but do not see how God is answering.

At the time Ben came home we were in between churches. In the early years of Cornerstone, the school met in the gym at a local Assembly of God church. We had become friends with Pastor Peters and his wife. They had four boys and were a great family. Sunday came and I felt that God wanted me to take Ben to hear Pastor Peters. I could trust him with my precious treasure.

That morning Pastor Peters had no idea that we would be there. His sermon was on the prodigal son. Ben told me later that he wanted to go to the altar but didn't want to be the only one, so he told God he would go forward if someone else went first. Someone else did go first—so Ben went forward and God saved him. He later asked about the other person who went forward, but no one remembered another seeker at the altar. God sometimes sends an angel to answer our prayer.

Ben and Tiffiny met again while Ben visited the mission in Santa Cruz and started dating again. It wasn't long before they were married. When they first met, Ben was looking for a "sinner girl"—but of course, God had the last laugh!

14

BRAGGING ON GOD

In the introduction I asked the question "Why do our children, even those raised in church, rebel and run to embrace evil?" I have attempted to answer this question many different times during my life as a parent.

When my parents heard me say in my testimony as a newly saved person that I was not raised in a Christian home, they were very hurt and offended that I would say such a thing. My mother especially felt that she had had raised me in a Christian home. We were referring to a Christian home with two very different definitions. What I meant was that I did not remember ever reading the Bible or praying as a family when I was growing up. I did not know what salvation was or how to find it.

What she meant was that she had worked hard to teach me good morals and values and to give me a happy home. We even went to church occasionally on holidays, and I was raised to know right from wrong and believe in God. Her definition did not help me when I reached the teen years and needed a God who could give me strength and purpose. It was not enough.

The easy answer to my "why" question for the good person who raises his or her children to be moral and know right from wrong is that not having God at the center of a home leaves our children wide open to the pitfalls of growing up with no God. They are on their own trying to figure life out.

But what about those of us who have children who were raised where there is prayer, Bible reading, church, and every other spiritual opportunity? When Andrew walked away from our home, I analyzed our shortcomings, our Christian walk, and our church. I beat myself up and felt like a total failure as a parent. But the story wasn't over.

At ages twenty-six and twenty-five, Steve and I found ourselves with four strong-willed, boisterous boys. Then Daniel was born seven years after Mark, so I was now thirty-two with five boys. To say that we were unprepared to be parents would be a gross understatement.

For the first few years after we became Christians, Steve was in a fog coming out of the drugs and the confusion of his early life. I came from a happy childhood experience but was raised with no spiritual influence. I prayed many times telling God that I didn't know how to raise children. I asked Him in prayer to help us and make up the difference. "O God," I prayed, "take our ignorance and mistakes and make up the difference in their lives." He did!

After reading my story you are probably wondering how, with five boys raised in such a crazy home, any of them survived. We moved almost every two years during the early years of their lives, we always had eccentric, sometimes crazy, unsaved people around them, and they were raised in a church where most of their activities were restricted by the rules of the church. God has been faithful to each of our sons, and today they are amazing men.

Matthew is an ordained elder and senior pastor of Vista (California) Family Church. He and Missy, his wife, are both working to complete doctorates in their fields. Missy is the administrator of a local Christian school.

Andrew was a Marine in Operation Restore Hope and completed his doctorate at Liberty University in educational leadership. He currently serves as a principal at a charter school and teaches a children's Sunday School class at his church. He and his wife, Leidy, live in Arizona.

Benjamin has a master of arts degree in leadership in the emergency management area from Grand Canyon University and has worked as a fire chief and in wildfire fire management. He lives in Dewey, Arizona, and is currently called to prayer for revival.

Mark is the cofounder of Samaritan Aviation, a missionary ministry to Papua New Guinea. He answered the missionary call that he received as a teenager. He and his wife, Kirsten, pioneered Christian work in Wewak, Papua New Guinea. He is a missionary pilot and mechanic. God has grown the ministry, which now has three float planes with pilots, mechanics, and medical missionaries. (Check them out at samaritanaviation. org.)

Daniel has a master of arts degree from York St. John University in England. He works in international education and was the director of international education at Northern Arizona University and the University of Arizona. He currently is the founder and owner of Catalina Global, a business to create international partnerships with universities in the United States and abroad. He currently lives with his wife, Lily, in Tucson, Arizona. Recently Lily received her master of arts degree from Harvard University.

We have so many grandchildren that I have to keep a spreadsheet to remember their birthdays. All our boys are in ministry in their local churches and abroad. I am blessed and know that God is helping all of us to "work out our salvation." They have all become people I would like even if they weren't related to me. God did it. He made up the difference!

15

MAKING SENSE OF IT ALL

Reading over the stories I have written makes me ask the questions "What does it mean?" and "What are the lessons learned?" The God stories in my life are a brief picture of a fleeting life on earth. They are stories of another time in history. They are not so much stories of my life as they are stories of *God in* my life!

Today we face circumstances that are different and yet the same. "Jesus Christ is the same yesterday, today, and forever" (Hebrews 13:8 NKJV). In my yesterday I learned about the power of prayer, the miracles that come from truly loving our neighbors, and the importance of staying honest with God and ourselves.

Looking back to my very beginnings in my Christian walk, I see the power of prayer. I believe that the prayers of a handful of people changed the lives of the hundreds of young people who wandered through the pages of the Shepherd's Fold and Elm Street Mission story.

Those who prayed did not remotely resemble those being prayed for. They did not understand the experiences of the young people they helped. They were not rebels, drug addicts, or questioning wanderers asking the question that Pontius Pilate asked, "What is truth?" These ordinary people knew an extraordinary God.

Brother Dozier was an example of a man who prayed. He was a very old man in the Santa Cruz church. He wasn't well physically, and I don't even remember talking with him that often. He prayed hours every day for the hippies God was sending to the little home church gathering in Wally and Beverly's front room. When Brother Dozier died, the doctor remarked to his wife that he had calluses on his knees and wondered why such an old man would have calluses there.

Beverly and Wally had both worked and saved to buy their home in the Santa Cruz Mountains that would later be named "Glory Hill." When we first met them, Beverly was a homemaker and stay-at-home mom. Wally drove to Verian, a manufacturing business in Palo Alto. It took him an hour each way in California traffic. Beverly was the prayer warrior and Wally the provider.

I think we prayed more then. Included in church services was a time of corporate prayer. We held prayer meetings in which people actually prayed. (Today we tend to talk longer than we pray.) For Christians it was taught that daily prayer and Bible study were requirements of a holy life. We couldn't wait to go to church and fellowship with other believers.

Today I hear people amazed at the idea of going to church Sunday mornings, Sunday nights, and Wednesday nights, as if it must really be a drag to go to church that much. Not only that, but also once or twice a year we had revival services that lasted a week or two and week-long camp meeting in the summers. We didn't attend the special meetings only when they fit into our schedules—we went every night. The first revival services we attended were in San Leandro, California, a sixty-seven-mile trip each way from Santa Cruz. Steve would get off work, we would eat dinner, change clothes, and drive a car full of people to the services. We went every night and twice on Sunday.

Camp meeting was held in southern California. We would take our vacation and drive the 450 miles to the camp. Then we would sleep in a tent, cabin, or dorm for a week and attend services three times a day. It was a time set aside to seek the Lord and fellowship with other Christians from around our district.

I am not saying that this is a formula for success or that we should replicate the methods of another time—I'm simply saying we prayed more.

Because we prayed, there was an attitude of love and caring about other people. We were looking for miracles around the next corner. We just knew that if God could save *us,* there were other people out there who needed to be changed as well. We believed that people would want the gospel message if they only knew about it.

Miracles are defined as supernatural healings or events. I have always looked at a miracle happening when a life is changed. It is a miracle when a person who is lost and feels hopeless puts his or her life into the hands of God and is changed and forgiven. It is a supernatural event in the life of that individual. A true experience of salvation is more than a casual acknowledgment of "accepting Jesus"—true salvation changes us totally, from the inside out.

I remember a time when someone asked Steve if he was sure the religion thing and belief in God weren't all in his head. He said, "I don't think that something that's all in my head and not real could stay there this long." We do not have the power to change ourselves and be delivered from the sins in our lives. Only God can work that miracle.

The idea of loving your neighbor as yourself was a real love that caused us to look for the people to whom God wanted us to be ministering, even if they weren't like us.

One of the final lessons of my yesterday is that I must keep honest with God and with myself. To think we can hide anything from God is silly. Acknowledging who we are keeps us honest. I have been a Christian now for over thirty years. It would be easy just to settle into the church routine. Being a respectable citizen, a faithful church lady, and a clean-living individual does not make me a Christian.

I cannot rest in my own goodness. To keep my first love faith alive, I must be watchful of my heart and attitudes. When I am wrong I need to admit it. When I am wronged I need to forgive. To stay alive spiritually I must pray, read God's Word, fellowship with other Christians, keep loving my neighbor, and stay honest with God.

I pray that this abbreviated story of my life will make you laugh, pray, and be determined to live close to God.

To God and to you—*I lift up my soul!*

ABOUT THE AUTHOR

SANDY LAMPSON PALM was born in Albany, California. She was raised in the California Bay Area, where she attended elementary school and graduated from Irvington High School in Fremont, California.

After becoming a Christian, her husband was called into ministry and Sandy became a pastor's wife for twenty-five years. Together they ran the Elm Street Mission in Santa Cruz, California, for seven years.

When her five sons were old enough for her to work toward her education goals, she returned to complete her college degree, graduating first from San Jose State University with a bachelor of arts degree in history. She later earned a master of arts degree in English rhetoric and composition and a doctor of education degree in curriculum and instruction from Northern Arizona University in Flagstaff, Arizona.

She has worked in numerous teaching and administration positions beginning with teaching history and English as a secondary school instructor. She has served as a dean of education, Christian school principal, and professor and is currently director of general education at Nazarene Bible College.

Sandy and her husband, Steve, live in the Prescott, Arizona, area and attend Prescott Church of the Nazarene.

Made in the USA
Columbia, SC
01 April 2025

56012951R00080